We're All Okay:
A Millenial's Treatise

Decoding the Country's Biggest Non-Mystery

Michelle Petrazzuolo, SPHR, SHRM-SCP

Introduction

If you are among the thousands of business owners and senior leaders who have thrown your hands up in frustration trying to understand Millennials, you only have yourselves to blame.

Yes, it's harsh, but it's true. There has been a lot written about Millennials – a quick Google search for the term in their News section yielded 3,340,000 results in half a second. Much has been said about Millennials, as well. In conferences and workshops across the nation, this cohort that is both feared and coveted in the workplace has been the hot topic. The subject has been done to death.

With one exception. Why aren't Millennials doing any of the talking? At the time of this writing, just one of Amazon's top ten books on the generation were written by a member of it, but only as a co-author with a Traditionalist. Often these books do more to reinforce the preconceived notions that some people hold rather than challenging them, with titles that frighten (*When Millennials Take Over*) or disdain (*What's Wrong With Millennials?*). This is where the responsibility of learning begins – in order to truly understand something, you need to be willing to have your preconceived notions dismantled, but it is often easier to read a pearl-clutching perspective of how terrible we are rather than trying to see the world from our perspective.

Mind you, this is not to discount the content and intentions of these authors or works, but if they were able to help us unlock this so-called mystery, they would have already done it. Maybe instead of talking *about* Generation Y we start talking *to* them. That is exactly my intention with this book.

I think the person who put it best is Shane Smith, founder of Vice Magazine, a decidedly non-traditional media outlet for journalism that is both groundbreaking (they were the ones who documented Dennis Rodman's trip to North Korea) and wildly interesting to young readers. When asked how he did it, he was blunt: "These kids have been marketed to since they were babies. They've developed the most sophisticated bullshit detectors in history...hand over your company to the interns, because there's no way you can reverse-engineer it."[1]

Many people choose to get their impressions about Generation Y from the media. The popular HBO program *Girls* comes to mind. It follows four women in their twenties in New York, and catalogs their experiences with relationships and in social situations. The women are not role models, nor do I believe they were meant to be. They don't seem to have many well-balanced relationships with friends or lovers, and their casual use of a collection of various drugs is not unheard of, but I'd argue it's also not the norm. While I don't think the show was meant to be a diorama of Millennial life – in many ways it was autobiographical for the show's creator, Lena Dunham[2] - members of the generations before us have taken it as such, and if that is how you've gotten your view of what my generation is like, I'm not surprised if you can't stand us. I myself can't stand the ladies on the show, and I'm not alone as a Millennial who is open about not being represented by the people on the program.[3] The conversation has gotten out of control.

_____

[1] Beltrone, G. (2013, March 24). Vice CEO Punches Back at Critics of North Korea Trip. Retrieved July 2, 2015, from http://www.adweek.com/news/television/vice-ceo-punches-back-critics-north-korea-trip-148111

[2] Goldberg, L. (2012, January 13). TCA: Lena Dunham Says HBO's 'Girls' Isn't 'Sex and the City' Retrieved October 25, 2015, from http://www.hollywoodreporter.com/live-feed/tca-hbo-girls-lena-dunham-judd-apatow-281483

[3] Kasperkevic, J. (2012, April 20). Why Millennials Are Nothing Like The 'Girls' On

I was speaking to a business owner recently who said that she didn't even bother to hire any young workers anymore. They didn't have a good work ethic, and they would only stick around as long as it took for them to find a better paycheck. How unfortunate for her, I replied, because with the right approach not only could you find and retain great young workers at your company, but a motivated Millennial will bring unparalleled passion to the job, and internalize your company's work in a way that other generations have not matched.

I tend to get angry when I read what older generations have to say about us. Yes, we are different. Very different, I'll even say. But why is it that the differences that we note in those that are older than us are traits we need to learn and accept to get along in the workplace, and everything that makes my generation unique, challenging and enigmatic is wrong? I can't blame anyone specifically for this, because people have been shocked by younger folks for centuries. As Lord Ashley stated in the British House of Commons in 1843, "The morals of the children are tenfold worse than formerly."[4]

The time to remove the veil from this subject is now, as Millennials now comprise about half of the workforce, and by 2030 will be 75% of it.[5] Companies have spent countless dollars in an attempt to attract and engage this generation, with mixed results. In addition to simply bringing understanding to the topic, I will also make suggestions on how to increase engagement and retention of this group without having to break the bank or reinvent the wheel.

As the founder of a Workplace Generations business resource group, I've had a numerous of conversations with people with the

---

HBO's Show. Retrieved October 25, 2015, from http://www.businessinsider.com/i-am-not-a-lena-dunham-millennial-2012-4
[4] Condition And Education Of The Poor. (n.d.). Retrieved October 26, 2015, from http://hansard.millbanksystems.com/commons/1843/feb/28/condition-and-education-of-the-poor
[5] Mitchell, A. (2013, August 16). The Rise of the Millennial Workforce | WIRED. Retrieved April 30, 2015.

intention of changing hearts and minds. Some of the things I've brought up during these talks are surprising. Others are not very shocking at all, if it had been considered with context. For example – why would we be loyal to one company for our entire careers when that worked out quite poorly for our parents? We'll talk about that further in Chapter Three. Small revelations like these will not only help to illuminate a mysterious subject, but hopefully demonstrate how to think critically about the information we are given about a group of people, rather than simply accepting someone else's experience as truth.

Through research, analysis and a bit of anecdotal storytelling, I hope to bring clarity to a subject that has been touted as a great enigma, but probably should never have been in the first place.

The Players

"The youth now love luxury. They have bad manners, contempt for authority." –Socrates

In order to give ourselves a common background from which to speak, let's spend some time talking about who, exactly, are the generations that will be referenced throughout this book. It should be noted that different sources provide different dates to encapsulate the generations, and there is no official date range that is used by any organization. The dates given are gathered from the Pew Research Center[6] and represent commonly used parameters. In addition, many individuals that were born during one generation identify more strongly to another, especially for those born on the cusp of two. This identity may have arisen from who the individual was raised by or other factors in their background, and is an important consideration in understanding these groups.

Traditionalists

Also known as the Silent Generation, Traditionalists are those born between 1928 and 1945. This is the oldest generation in the workforce at this time, and represents workers who are eligible and ready to retire, or who have chosen to continue working past retirement age, either for self-fulfillment or due to financial stresses.

---

[6] The Generations Defined. (2014, March 5). Retrieved April 30, 2015, from http://www.pewsocialtrends.org/2014/03/07/millennials-in-adulthood/sdt-next-america-03-07-2014-0-06/

Baby Boomers

These individuals were born between 1946 and 1964, and are a very large cohort. This group is entering the last stage of their careers, with some already past retirement age, and the youngest members still ten to fifteen years away from that milestone. This group is currently being outpaced as a percentage of representation of the workforce by Millennials.

Generation X

The first of the lettered generations, this group was born between 1965 and 1980, and represents about a quarter of the workforce. These individuals are in the mid-career phase, although more are joining the trend to leave one career for a second with plenty of working years remaining.

Millennials

This generation, also known as Generation Y, represents individuals born between 1980 and 2000. The older members of this generation may have well-established careers at this time, or may still be struggling to find a footing due to economic pressures. The youngest of this cohort are in their college years or preparing to enter college at a time when justifying the expense and value of a degree is becoming more difficult.

Generation Z

While this generation is not yet in the workforce, they are worth mentioning. These individuals were born after 2000, and while the oldest of them are teenagers, there is much yet to learn about what this group will be like and what they will do as they enter the workforce. It will be informative to observe the current historical context under which they are being raised as we seek to get to know them going forward.

History is the most important key to understanding any generation, including Millennials. As the Arab proverb goes, "People resemble their times more than they resemble their parents." Perhaps this is what is so frustrating for many of us in that generation – our history was your present. It seems that some people have poor memories.

For now, let's take some time to review the major historical factors of previous generations that informed who they became as workers, as this perspective will be the foundation upon which our understanding of Generation Y will be built.

Economic Repercussions and the Traditionalists

The economic roller coaster that defined much of the first half of the 21st Century is the backdrop for this generation. The stock market crash of 1929[7] began an era of stark poverty for most of the country, a time when jobs and resources were hard to come by. If one was going to survive this time, it was going to take very hard work and sacrifice, and that is what many did. Young traditionalists saw their parents break their backs to make ends meet, and eventually many of these children also went into the workforce to provide for their families. This is surely the beginning of one of the hallmarks of the Traditionalist in the workplace – a willingness to work hard and get the job done, even when it is difficult or unpleasant.

By 1933 a weary nation was in need of swift action, and the election of Franklin Roosevelt was the catalyst. Many of the employment laws that are in effect today are thanks to his presidency, and also provided definition to this generation. The establishment of the rights of workers to unionize and bargain collectively were established by the National Industrial Recovery Act of 1933, strengthened later by the Wagner National Labor Relations Act of 1935, and perhaps it is because of

---

[7] Timeline of the Great Depression. (n.d.). Retrieved April 30, 2015, from http://www.pbs.org/wgbh/americanexperience/features/timeline/rails-timeline/

this historical context that union membership rates are highest among the oldest workers.[8]

Two years later, in 1935, Roosevelt passes the Social Security Act,[9] meaning workers could work for their entire lives with the security that they would be taken care of upon their retirement. These policies and many others, collectively known as the New Deal, created an economy that struggled to succeed until the start of World War II. Indeed, the war itself created a sense of duty and purpose among the population that this generation brings to the workplace, built on sacrifice and doing what is difficult because it is right.

Throughout their working lives, and even today, this generation has brought their unique perspective to their jobs and shaped their work environments. According to a white paper published by AARP, Traditionalists view work as a privilege, and treat it that way.[10] Bending over backwards to get something done for the company isn't something special – it's how you should do the job every day. Once you find a job that pays the bills, there is no reason to have to look for another one. It's not hard to imagine why the Millennial tendency to spend only a few years (at most) in a role might irritate this generation. It would be equally difficult for them to understand why we are seeking to create a career path the very moment we walk in the door, or how we are already bringing ideas for innovation to a meeting when we've not earned the right to do so yet through our time and sweat equity.

This generation does not expect recognition or rewards for their work. The paycheck is the reward and it will be sufficient for them every

[8] Bureau of Labor Statistics. (2015). Union Membership – 2014 [Press Release]. Retrieved from http://www.bls.gov/news.release/pdf/union2.pdf

[9] Timeline of the Great Depression. (n.d.). Retrieved April 30, 2015, from http://www.pbs.org/wgbh/americanexperience/features/timeline/rails-timeline/

[10] American Association of Retired Persons. (2007). *Leading a Multigenerational Workforce*. Retrieved from http://assets.aarp.org/www.aarp.org_/articles/money/employers/leading_multigenerational_workforce.pdf

time. They are unlikely to speak up if they lack something that they want or need because they will either learn to live without it or find a way to work around it. That ingenuity has been invaluable for businesses, and it's why these individuals are still able to bring their talents and expertise to their jobs, whether it's a fulfilling volunteer role or a post-retirement challenge.

Seasons of Change for Baby Boomers

Whereas Traditionalists were never ones to rock a boat unless necessary, Baby Boomers seem to have perfected the tactic. They came of age during a time when war was losing its place in our country's history as a unifier and instead creating significant divisions, even within families. Nothing was taken for granted, and no status quo was left unquestioned.

Counterculture began in 1947 with the Roswell incident, which spurred a flurry of UFO reports across the nation, not so surprisingly coinciding with significant leaps forward in aeronautical technology for the United States military. Intercontinental flights became more common in this era, and once distant lands were now reachable for the ordinary citizen. Conflicts in far-off countries were suddenly brought much closer to our backyard, so when the Soviet Union detonates their first atomic bomb in 1949, the distance doesn't provide much comfort. As each side of the Cold War escalates the rhetoric and their corresponding actions, the nation is brought to the brink and suddenly peace seems like a goal worth prioritizing. [11]

At home during this time, the Department of Labor widens its work under the direction of Maurice Tobin. Even in the early 50's his support of the Fair Employment Practices Bill demonstrated the need to protect people's right to seek employment and be treated equally.[12]

---

[11] Timeline of the Boomer Generation. (2014, July 31). Retrieved June 23, 2015, from http://www.pbs.org/wnet/americanmasters/episodes/the-boomer-list/timeline-of-a-generation/3153/

Sadly, this would not come to fruition until over a decade later, after the challenges of the desegregation and civil rights movements. Social action was front-and-center in helping people promote change to injustice, and it became the platform upon which the huge social change of this era was built.

This generation witnessed many tragedies, from the assassinations of President Kennedy and Martin Luther King, Jr. to the horrors of the Vietnam War. People found their voices, engaging in actions that urged the fight for peace and equal treatment for all citizens.

This was also, however a time of great accomplishments. Americans went first to space, then to the moon. Perhaps one of the most important pieces of legislation for the nation and the workplace, the Civil Rights Act of 1964, was passed. Discrimination on the basis of race or sex was no longer permitted, and this became the cornerstone of employment policy for decades to come.[13] The Equal Pay Act of 1963, Age Discrimination in Employment act of 1967 and the Occupational Safety and Health Act of 1970 were also passed during this era, and still play a significant role in the treatment of workers today, informing daily Human Resources decisions.[14] So much of what we rely upon today as the standards of how to treat employees was because of these crucial pieces of legislation.

In a word, this generation was groundbreaking. They were Time Magazine's Man of the Year in 1967 – the entire cohort (quite a difference from Generation Y – we got a rather unflattering portrayal in their now-infamous "Me Me Me" cover in May of 2013 [below]). They fought hard

---

[12] The U.S. Department of Labor Timeline – Alternate version. (n.d.). Retrieved June 24, 2015, from
http://www.dol.gov/100/timeline/alternate.version.timeline.html
[13] Timeline of the Boomer Generation. (2014, July 31). Retrieved June 23, 2015, from http://www.pbs.org/wnet/americanmasters/episodes/the-boomer-list/timeline-of-a-generation/3153/
[14] The U.S. Department of Labor Timeline – Alternate version. (n.d.). Retrieved June 24, 2015, from
http://www.dol.gov/100/timeline/alternate.version.timeline.html

to make sure that everyone had a voice, so it should come as no surprise that Baby Boomers are exceptional teammates and team builders for a company. Unlike Traditionalists, these employees are happy to challenge the status quo.[15]

This generation will surely revolutionize each step of their lives, including retirement. The group that is shaping what it means to be in your golden years in the modern age is not resting on their laurels. They are taking the opportunity to enjoy different work, volunteer, or take adventurous trips that make us think of anything but grandparents. These people still know how to rock – after all, they invented it.

---

[15] American Association of Retired Persons. (2007). *Leading a Multigenerational Workforce*. Retrieved from http://assets.aarp.org/www.aarp.org_/articles/money/employers/leading_multig enerational_workforce.pdf

This generation experienced dashed expectations in many ways. The generation that came before laid the foundation for continued prosperity and hope, and many of the circumstances of the Generation X era led to disappointment. Women's liberation was, along with a number of other causes, meant to ensure that anyone could choose to work or pursue education without limitations due to gender. An unintended product of this movement meant that divorces became much more common, and young people were increasingly living in single-parent homes, or had relatives who were splitting the traditional family unit. A government that had engendered cooperation and sacrifice of previous generations through fighting for the greater good now bred distrust, thanks to the end of the Vietnam War and the scandal-beset Nixon administration. Events that were meant to bring great pride and accomplishment failed, such as the Three Mile Island and Chernobyl disasters.

The workplace in this era was challenging for many. An economic downturn in 1979 spurred layoffs across the nation, followed eight years later by a stock market crash in 1987. [16] Many found themselves unemployed, leading to the passage of the Worker Adjustment and Retraining Notification Act in 1988, intended to help workers be better prepared in the event of mass layoffs or plant closings.[17] Having grown up in such tumultuous times, it is understandable that a Generation X worker likes order, stability and structure.[18]

---

[16] Ibid.

[17] The U.S. Department of Labor Timeline – Alternate version. (n.d.). Retrieved June 24, 2015, from http://www.dol.gov/100/timeline/alternate.version.timeline.html

[18] American Association of Retired Persons. (2007). *Leading a Multigenerational Workforce*. Retrieved from http://assets.aarp.org/www.aarp.org_/articles/money/employers/leading_multigenerational_workforce.pdf

As is the case with many people, struggle creates strength. Generation X, the smallest workforce generation, learned how to be self-sufficient. When asked what they are looking for most in this stage of their careers, this group says the opportunity to grow,[19] expecting that they will be able to create opportunities for themselves and take advantage of them. They are considered excellent problem-solvers, adaptable, and best equipped to manage others. [20]

No one likes being spoken about badly – I think we can all agree this is a cross-generational trait. This is often what happens, though, when people talk about Millennials, both in hushed office conversations and, just as often, to our faces. Let me share a true story of a conversation I experienced.

I attended a Diversity and Inclusion conference a couple of years ago, hosted by a leading business resource group organization. As a kickoff to the three-day event, they brought in a guest speaker to talk about diversity. He had written a book about how to speak differently about the subject, and brought a few great challenges to the table that made a group of diversity-minded professionals think critically about the job we are doing on workplace inclusion. It was a great topic to get the conference started.

One thought that he shared that really got me thinking was about right-handed privilege. Without even knowing it, the world is made for us right-handers. Doors open with our dominant hand. All scissors are made

[19] Job Seeker Nation Study: inside the Mind Of the Modern Job Seeker. (2015). Retrieved June 23, 2015 , from http://www.jobvite.com/wp-content/uploads/2015/01/jobvite_jobseeker_nation_2015.pdf
[20] Younger managers rise in the ranks: Survey quantifies management shift and reveals challenge, preferred workplace perks, and perceived generational strengths and weaknesses. (n.d.) Retrieved June 24, 2015, from http://www.multivu.com/mnr/63068-ernst-and-young-llp-research-younger-managers-rise-in-the-ranks

for us by default; to get a scissor that a left handed person can use requires a special order. It's so natural to us that it doesn't even bear our notice that there are people in the world who have a very different experience. It was eye-opening.

About halfway through the talk an audience member asked him about Millennials. It's a hot topic, and she was curious to know his perspective about what they are like and what they expect from their employers. To my dismay, he trotted out many of the same tropes that I will talk about in this chapter: they want to be rewarded for every little thing they do. They expect to rise to the top quickly and become disappointed when they don't. They give up easily.

It was hard to sit and listen to, not only because I felt that that wasn't really true (if only a partial explanation), but it was a set of lazy clichés. For a talk that was challenging us to think differently, we were being fed the same tired lines. Not only that, but we were talked about as if there were none of us in the room. Why does no one consider simply turning to us and asking?

It didn't take long before I raised my hand. "Out of curiosity," I asked, "could those of us who are actually Millennials in the audience raise our hands?" There were perhaps five of us out of two hundred. We were a small minority in the room, but we didn't deserve to be treated as if we were the elephant therein. I expressed my disappointment in what felt like my Norma Rae moment, and asked my fellow cohort if they felt as if what was being said about them was true. We all agreed that it was not. Wouldn't it be more fruitful to talk to us than around us, I asked?

Looking back, challenging a keynote speaker in front of his room presented a challenge to him that was pretty unfair. Having spent much of my career facilitating trainings and speaking publicly, to lose the trust and engagement of the room makes your job significantly more difficult. I was hoping he would address my concerns and perhaps give us a perspective that I hadn't already heard, but he did not. He explained away his

10

statements, rendering them essentially moot, and failed to advance the conversation at all.

I passed my card to the event organizers and offered to lead their next Millennial discussion. I have yet to hear from them.

That memory is quintessentially Generation Y. A young, inexperienced upstart throwing a wrench into a perfectly good seminar when I hadn't earned the right to do so. The response was equivalent to what many of us experience in the workplace: focus on the action rather than the potential gain. Imagine how everyone in that room might have enhanced their capacity to manage this generation if the conversation had gone differently, taken head-on.

It is important to take some time to review these well-known myths to both highlight the barriers that exist to understanding, but also to dig deeper into why they came into being in the first place. While the falsehoods are misleading, the soil in which they grew is filled with facts that all of us, including those of us in the generation, should address.

Myth #1: Millennials are Disloyal

It is an unassailable fact that the members of Generation Y feel no necessity to give their entire career to a willing employer. In fairness, it is rare that anyone could find the kind of job security that would allow them to spend thirty-five or more years with one company, but that is a far leap from where we are actually standing. On average, Millennials spend 4.4 years at each job.[21] If we spend forty years working before retirement, we could easily be at ten different companies in that time. I don't imagine we'll be getting gold watches at our farewell parties.

---

[21] Meister, J. (2012, August 14). Job Hopping Is the 'New Normal' for Millennials: Three Ways to Prevent a Human Resource Nightmare. Retrieved June 23, 2015, from http://www.forbes.com/sites/jeannemeister/2012/08/14/job-hopping-is-the-new-normal-for-millennials-three-ways-to-prevent-a-human-resource-nightmare/

Myth #2: Millennials Are Needy

Or self-centered. Or entitled. The most common example people point to is going to their child's soccer game and seeing a table of trophies – enough for both teams. Even the losers get prizes, they mutter, and it's not a very good lesson. In fact, the controversial Aspen Education Group asserts that we have too much self-esteem (which I am not convinced is something you can have too much of), and that the constant praise our generation received resulted in narcissism and 'deeply embedded entitlement'.[22] I do recall watching a lot of Sesame Street that said I was great and special.

Myth #3: Millennials Are Unmotivated

According to recent census statistics, nearly one-third of us are still living with our parents.[23] The meme of the neckbeard basement-dweller (below) comes to mind as we ponder such a huge percentage of a generation that didn't bother to get a decent job, earn a living and get their own places. Home ownership among the generation stands at historically low levels.[24]

---

[22] Narcissistic and Entitled to Everything! Does Gen Y Have Too Much Self-Esteem? (n.d.). Retrieved June 23, 2015, from http://aspeneducation.crchealth.com/articles/article-entitlement/

[23] Meyer, A. (2015, February 17). Census Bureau: 30.3% Millennials Still Living With Their Parents. Retrieved June 23, 2015, from http://www.cnsnews.com/news/article/ali-meyer/census-bureau-303-millennials-still-living-their-parents

[24] 15 Economic Facts About Millennials. (2014, October). Retrieved June 23, 2015,

Myth #4: Millennials Are Ungrateful

This is another symptom of the worker who hops from job to job, looking for their next better paycheck or opportunity. If a promotion isn't coming our way within a year or so of our arrival, we'll be looking elsewhere for our next step. At least a third of Generation Y workers see their current role as a stepping stone to their next role.[25] Considering that the average time spent at a job is 4.4 years, it's not taking a lot of time for Millennials to make this realization. Even worse, many may be entering the job with that perspective already.

Myth #5: Millennials Want Everything

Companies that attract this generation are usually mentioned in the same breath as the amazing perks that are offered. Google is an easy example of this – three delicious, chef-prepared meals per day, on-site car washes and all the snacks you can get your hands on. Companies are being forced to look for new ways to engage these workers and entice them to stay. One company is offering what they call "Pre-Cations", where newly-hired workers are given two weeks of paid time off before they walk in the door so they can be refreshed and ready to work on day one.[26] It's enough to inspire fury in some.

Myth #6: Millennials Are Digital Addicts

This is a myth only in a sense. Truly, our generation loves to be connected. According to Nielsen, eighty-five percent of us own

from
https://www.whitehouse.gov/sites/default/files/docs/millennials_report.pdf
[25] Job Seeker Nation Study: inside the Mind Of the Modern Job Seeker. (2015). Retrieved June 23, 2015 , from http://www.jobvite.com/wp-content/uploads/2015/01/jobvite_jobseeker_nation_2015.pdf
[26] Faw, L. (2015, April 15). For Millennials, Is a "Pre-Cation" the Next Big Perk? Retrieved June 23, 2015, from
http://www.cornerstoneondemand.com/blog/millennials-pre-cation-next-big-perk#.VYoA-Czs34Y

smartphones.[27] We coined the term FOMO (Fear Of Missing Out) to describe why it's so tempting to check for Twitter updates so frequently. Where this becomes a myth, however, is that this addiction causes our work product or commitment to suffer, and we will explore this in a later chapter. I'll also state for the record that our generation is not the only one to suffer from FOMO. What happens if you hear about something major the day after it occurs? You've already missed being a part of the conversation on social media. All the best memes are already created and viral. News outlets suffer the same problem, as being second to break a story just isn't good enough. This has resulted in some rather odd mistaken headlines, such as murder suspect Robert Durst being confused with Fred Durst, lead singer of the 90's era nu-metal band Limp Bizkit, who not only didn't murder anyone, but hadn't been in the news for quite some time.

So, where do we go from here? Over the next few chapters I will explore each of these myths in depth, talk about where the information is correct and why some incorrect conclusions have been drawn. I will also make best practice recommendations on how to adjust your business to make the most of these workers. There is a significant potential to be tapped here, and the companies that do so will be miles ahead of their less-prepared competitors.

But wait…What about Generation Z?

We are so undecided on this generation that we haven't even given them their own name yet. I hope we've come up with a new labelling scheme by the time the following generation is ready to be titled, as we have run out of alphabet! In a later chapter we will take the time to review the zeitgeist that this group is experiencing now, and provide some predictions on what will be meaningful to them, as well as what will engage them in the workplace.

---

[27] Mobile Millennials: Over 85% of Generation Y Owns Smartphones. (2014, September 50. Retrieved June 23, 2015, from http://www.nielsen.com/us/en/insights/news/2014/mobile-millennials-over-85-percent-of-generation-y-owns-smartphones.html

Myth #1: Millennials Are Disloyal

"Will this emerging generation of leaders ever care as much as we did about building careers? And, if not, what does that mean for business?" – *Patricia Sellers, Fortune Magazine*

Loyalty is, on its face, a virtue. Demonstrating a commitment to someone, or in our case some company, shows a sense of honor and respect for the bosses who employed you. Knowing that the person you hire for a job is going to stick around for you to get a return on your investment is understandable, particularly when some figures show replacing a lost employee can cost up to 21.4% of the role's salary.[28] If yours is a niche business requiring a select set of skills or experiences, you could end up paying more or, perhaps worse, compromising on quality just to fill the position. Getting people to stick around is good.

For a long time, this was not a difficult task. The members of the Traditionalists, as we noted before, were pleased to get a job and considered it a privilege. In fact, they considered building a career and legacy with one company throughout their entire working life as a point of pride.[29] Companies contributed to this by ensuring they took care of their

---

[28] Boushey, H. & Glynn, S. (2012, November 16). There Are Significant Business Costs to Replacing Employees. Retrieved June 27, 2015, from https://www.americanprogress.org/issues/labor/report/2012/11/16/44464/there-are-significant-business-costs-to-replacing-employees/

[29] Traditionalists, Baby Boomers, Generation X, Generation Y (and Generation Z) Working Together. (n.d.). Retrieved June 27, 2015, from http://www.un.org/staffdevelopment/pdf/Designing Recruitment, Selection & Talent Management Model tailored to meet UNJSPF's Business Development Needs.pdf

workers, offering pensions that would ensure retirees would continue to receive paychecks and healthcare through their golden years. As of 1980, a peak for pensions in the United States, forty-six percent of workers were covered this type of benefit.[30]

Cue the montage of familiar retirement party tableaus. Workers retiring after having served a company for forty years. A cake, balloons, a gold watch. A big dinner at a local restaurant where all of the retiree's co-workers, now close friends after decades working together, wish the celebrant well. Many of us may remember being invited to such a party for parents or grandparents, and it was easy to see that this person had become admired as a trusted colleague and experienced professional. We also know that with a few exceptions, we won't be seeing much of this anymore. It just isn't the way things go nowadays.

It's a common cliché, but a lazy one, to point to the generation that stubbornly refuses to give their entire career to one company as disloyal. I assure you, I hear your reply already: it's not just hoping someone will stay with an organization for a few decades, but even a few years. My argument is that this is not merely a symptom of a generation that demands instant gratification, but an economy that no longer supports the decision to remain with a company for more than five or so years at a time. For now, it is helpful to understand why there are practically no career-long employees anymore.

The changing face of retirement has caused many people to look at their plans differently. Pensions, once a wonderful nest egg one could rely on, have become so rare as to be a shocking benefit in a private organization. Whereas almost half of all workers could look forward to a pension in previous years, by 2008 that percentage dropped to twenty,[31]

---

[30] A Timeline of the Evolution of Retirement in the United States. (2010). Retrieved June 27, 2015, from http://scholarship.law.georgetown.edu/cgi/viewcontent.cgi?article=1049&context=legal

[31] Butrica, B., Iams, H., Smith, K., & Tober, E. (2009). The Disappearing Defined Benefit Pension and Its Potential Impact on the Retirement Incomes of Baby

and current figures show that the number of private companies that offer a pension dropped to eight percent by 2013. Why? The defined benefit plan, as it is known, is a risky investment. The company is on the hook to their employees whether they are able to pay or not, or despite the idea that this money could support the company better elsewhere in their balance book.[32]

It's a challenge for an organization to try to manage the future when it is tied up in pensions. Not only do they have the cost of paying the benefit to consider, but with people living longer now than ever, the total cost of having paid a pension rises dramatically. Factor in the economic uncertainty that came with the recent recession, some companies found that they simply couldn't pay, and those pensions got clawed back. Take the example of Detroit's city employees. Thousands of workers spent years in an organization that offered them a benefit that they could look forward to utilizing in their golden years. Now, due to mismanagement on the part of the city, these workers had to give back huge lump sums, up to $89,000 in one case, as part of a bankruptcy agreement the city negotiated.[33] The financial security they had once been promised was compromised. They played by a set of rules when they accepted the job, and the rules got changed when they were at their most vulnerable. Disloyalty, indeed.

The choice to change from defined benefit plans to defined contribution plans, the most popular of which being the 401(k), has been a rapidly-growing trend. It shifts the risk of these retirement dollars from a business to the employee, and the argument is often made that it helps

Boomers. Retrieved June 27, 2015, from
http://www.ssa.gov/policy/docs/ssb/v69n3/v69n3p1.html
[32] Rafter, D. (2013, September 26). What's killing the employee pension plan? Retrieved July 17, 2015, from http://www.money-rates.com/personal-finance/employee-pension-plans-disappear.htm.
[33] Tompor, S. (2015, January 16). Detroit pensioners decided if they'll pay upfront on clawback. Retrieved July 17, 2015, from http://www.freep.com/story/money/personal-finance/susan-tompor/2015/01/16/detroit-pensioners-lump-sum-clawback-susan-tompor/21829671/

employees manage their own money, allowing them to make smarter choices than perhaps their employer would. They could select one of a number of investment vehicles, from high-risk stock plans to interest-bearing money market accounts, and considering their own contributions, the individual had total control. No more reliance on a faceless monolith to manage your safety net.

Here's part of the problem: most people don't have the financial aptitude to fully understand these funds and strategically manage their money. Ask the average person to sit down and read a prospectus. In fact, I challenge you to do so. Read just one prospectus on a fund offered through your 401(k) and see if it makes sense to you. The sheer size of the book would be enough to deter a person, and when you consider there may be ten, twenty or more options in the plan, it's laughable. Someone coming home from a full day of work, having a meal, spending time with their families and attempting to get a good night's sleep will find the task impossible. Reading and understanding this material is a job on its own – it's known as a financial advisor.

As a result, a questionably well-intentioned shift of responsibility has created new problems. We are told repeatedly by advisors and economists to contribute enough to our 401(k) plan to receive the maximum employer match, which is great if your company offers one. Between 2010 and 2012, seven percent of companies stopped offering a match; even worse, between 2009 and 2013, six percent of companies stopped offering a 401(k) plan at all.[34] The advice also fails to take into account that the average worker's paycheck has not kept pace with the cost of living, and it's harder now than ever just to afford the basics. Contributing five percent of a salary to get the company's match, while a great proposal in theory, is impossible in reality for many families.

---

[34] Gladych, P. (2013, May 2). Fewer employers match 401(k) contributions. Retrieved July 17, 2015, from http://www.benefitspro.com/2013/05/02/fewer-employers-match-401k-contributions

It's also a fair question to ask whether the risk of a market-invested 401(k) plan is a sensible gamble. The recession of 2008 caused plenty of investors to lose thousands. I remember watching a financial advisor on television tell us not to jump ship from our accounts – don't look at your balances, they will bounce back. The worst thing we could do, evidently, was sell low, and it makes sense, unless you're on the precipice of retirement and your years of saving are suddenly down the tubes. What option do you have left?

Millennials have been watching. Many of us can think of parents or grandparents, in our own families or those of our friends, for whom retirement is just not an option. We've seen these same people giving their days, years and careers to their companies because they are loyal, dedicated workers, and it hasn't always worked out for them. So we turn to what we do best: hustle.

It is key to now explore how all of this history translates to an average job tenure of 4.4 years. For many Millennials starting out, both before and during the recession, the economic realities of establishing financial security were grim. The starting salaries for the Millennial workers compared to what they were for other generations at the same age were markedly lower, and were hit harder than those of our forebears during the 2008 recession.[35] We've also struggled with record high student loan debts,[36] so we have fewer resources with which to hit basic life milestones like home ownership. Figuring out how to make more money is crucial to our lifetime success.

---

[35] Kiersz, A. (2014, December 5). Millennials Aren't Making As Much As Their Parents Did When They Were Young. Retrieved July 17, 2015, from http://www.businessinsider.com/young-adult-vs-all-adult-weekly-earnings-2014-12

[36] Kasperkevic, J. (2013, December 6). Student loan debt hits a new high as millennials take 'poverty-wage' jobs. Retrieved July 17, 2015, from http://www.theguardian.com/money/us-money-blog/2013/dec/06/student-loan-debt-minimum-poverty-wage-jobs

As it turns out, changing jobs and moving to different companies makes more financial sense. The average raise for an employee for 2014 was three percent.[37] When you factor in an inflation rise of .8 percent, along with a 3.4 percent rise in food costs,[38] you start to feel as if you are actually losing money. Compare the average increase in salary a worker can expect to realize if they jump to another company – between ten and twenty percent. On top of that, one statistic shows that staying at the same company for more than two years at a time could reduce your lifetime earnings by up to fifty percent.[39] You would have to be a fool not to at least consider that going to another company might work out better for you in the long run. What would be the virtue of loyalty if it is at the expense of our ability to provide for ourselves and our families?

All of our hustling has paid off. Millennials participate in their 401(k) plans at a rate of seventy percent, and the generation started their savings earlier than any generation before them – at age twenty-two. We don't expect Social Security to be available to us by the time we reach the appropriate age, so we not only participate in our plans, but actively do so, leveraging the technology of apps and websites to view and change our plans as we see fit.[40] We know we are ultimately the ones who will take care of ourselves when we retire, so we'll handle it, thank you. This is a potential engagement tool for businesses who are willing and able to

---

[37] Keng, C. (2014, June 22). Employees Who Stay In Companies Longer Than Two Years Get Paid 50% Less. Retrieved July 17, 2015, from http://www.forbes.com/sites/cameronkeng/2014/06/22/employees-that-stay-in-companies-longer-than-2-years-get-paid-50-less/

[38] Annual US Inflation in 2014 Rises 0.8%. (2015, January 16). Retrieved July 17, 2015, from http://www.usinflationcalculator.com/inflation/annual-us-inflation-in-2014-rises-0-8/10001592/

[39] Keng, C. (2014, June 22). Employees Who Stay In Companies Longer Than Two Years Get Paid 50% Less. Retrieved July 17, 2015, from http://www.forbes.com/sites/cameronkeng/2014/06/22/employees-that-stay-in-companies-longer-than-2-years-get-paid-50-less/

[40] 15 facts about Millennials' retirement readiness...and 7 steps for long-term success. (2014, July 1). Retrieved July 17, 2015, from https://www.transamericacenter.org/docs/default-source/resources/center-research/tcrs2014_factsheet_millennials.pdf

indulge our desire for better financial management. Talk with your investment plan brokers and see what programs they have to offer for your employees. Have a financial advisor in for a lunchtime seminar, or a question-and-answer session. To bemoan low 401(k) participation is only half the battle; there are so many resources available through your broker relationship to bring to bear. Don't just give us a product and wish us the best – help us use it wisely.

The correlating downside of this is for businesses to bear. Employees who leave every few years are costly, not only in the real dollars it will take to replace them, but in the experience and knowledge walking out the door when they do. How should an organization compete? Surely it comes down to money, and I agree, to a point.

The money an employee makes in a job is considered a hygiene factor – meeting the obligations of hygiene factors doesn't do a lot to increase engagement, but when they are poor or absent they will drag motivation and loyalty down like nothing else. Not to mention, it's tough to compete on money. There will always be, with extremely rare exceptions, a company that is willing to pay more, and as we'll see in a later chapter, it eventually has diminishing returns. To enter an ever-escalating arms race of high salaries is not only a zero-sum game, but unsustainable. The landscape of business and the economy is in a state of high flux at this time, and throwing cash at a problem isn't going to be the smart way to weather the storm. Don't compete on money.

Instead, compete on future opportunity. After all, that is why Millennials are always looking for a new job. They are constantly on the lookout for the next step on their path to success. Don't immediately dismiss that – any good entrepreneur is doing the same for their business. We simply consider our careers our business. It may be that strategic drive that has created young billionaires like Mark Zuckerberg, Dustin Moskovitz and Sean Parker.

Rather than rolling their eyes at employees who are always looking for the bigger, better deal, companies with highly engaged workforces are participating in the discussion. An Adecco survey indicated as much as sixty-eight percent of Millennials cite development as a key factor in what they look for at work.[41] Taking the time to understand the career goals of workers bears fruit not only for that individual, but for the company as a whole. Rather than looking to an external candidate to fill a critical role, start developing that role's successor well before you lose the incumbent. Promoting from within preserves important institutional knowledge and helps maintain the culture.

I'll put forward a rather radical idea for how to tackle this problem, as well, for larger companies that can sustain it: plan for short-term employees. If the average worker is spending a few years at a company, use this to your advantage. Keep the knowledge flow moving at all times. Create a career path that will take up those four years so that you can plan the work around project timeframes rather than a "This Will Be the Situation Forever" approach. No worker should be so indispensable to a company that their departure would mean a department's, team's or even an entire business' downfall. If you've already fallen in to this trap, you must act quickly.

Once a worker moves into a position, the knowledge transfer begins from the more senior workers downward. The new worker assimilates this information, and then brings their own knowledge and experience into the role to innovate and improve work processes. As they themselves become more senior, bring a junior worker in below who can begin to take on the new systems the worker created. Bring new challenges to the now tenured employee, who can continue to grow and bring creativity to them. You may find that, rather than looking for the next move, this individual will instead be looking to you to find out what great new opportunities will be coming their way.

---

[41] Goudreau, J. (2013, March 7). 7 Surprising Ways To Motivate Millennial Workers. Retrieved July 17, 2015, from http://www.forbes.com/sites/jennagoudreau/2013/03/07/7-surprising-ways-to-motivate-millennial-workers/

Developing and deploying this type of infrastructure, or even a more common career path framework, takes work and, critically, high-level buy-in. If the organizational leaders aren't involved or interested in workers' development, it will show, and a discussion about a development plan will remain only that. There needs to be tangible results for a program to be truly impactful. A mentoring program is an excellent way to help individuals determine their next career steps and be a part of that conversation, but it should be carefully managed. At the outset, thoughtful consideration should be given to who would gain the most from mentoring, and where the payoffs would be the biggest for the company. Pair the mentee with a mentor who will help them enhance not only their own acumen, but how well they are performing their current role. Measure before the program begins the productivity and performance of the participants so you can see the gains once the program ends. Mentoring should benefit both the employee and the company.

Another key component of the development discussion is one that many managers avoid – where the employee isn't measuring up. I see this among supervisors often. It's easy to tell someone why they are doing a great job, so development discussions and performance appraisals often fall into the trap of being very complementary, but valueless. To really help an employee to get to the next level of their career, a manager needs to be willing to be honest about what's holding that employee back. Are they lacking education? Experience? Maybe it's not possible for that person to get the skills they need at your company. Be frank. Sure, that employee may leave as a result, but keeping someone around who isn't going to continue to deliver more year-on-year to your company is a slight for both parties.

On the other hand, having a frank discussion about deficiencies shouldn't just be a laundry list of what's missing in a person's work. To get the most out of an employee, pair that list with an equal list of how the worker can gain the skills noted and allow them to take the initiative. Provide a list of courses, projects or tasks, including some that the worker can take up on their own, and watch them work. The truly motivated will take that list and run with it, and in return for an extra half hour of work on your part, you'll get an employee who has surpassed their own expectations and accomplishes more than ever before.

This brings us to another myth about Millennials, and just in time. Millennials can't take constructive criticism. All they want to hear is how great they are. How can an authentic conversation even take place?

I'm glad you asked.

Myth #2: Millennials Are Needy

"You have to speak to them a little bit like a therapist on television might speak to a patient. You can't be harsh. You cannot tell them you're disappointed in them. You really can't ask them to live and breathe the company. Because they're living and breathing themselves and that keeps them very busy." –Marian Salzman

One of the best days of any elementary school year for many children, myself included, was an event we called Field Day. During Field Day the entire student body was organized into three teams, and various physical competitions were held on the big lawn outside. It was great exercise and the perfect way to spend the penultimate day of classes before summer break. At the end, every participant got a shiny ribbon to commemorate the occasion.

Yes, we all won. Everyone got a prize for Field Day. No one went home wishing they had something to proudly present to their parents – we all got to celebrate. It was a great feeling, but one that has been blamed for Millennials' need to constantly be told how great they are. We can't take criticism, and we want to know within our first couple of weeks how well we're doing.

It seems that the alarms are being rung not just for how Generation Y will ruin the workplace with their praise-seeking attitudes, but truly the entire fabric of society could be at risk. An actual letter written in to MoneyTalks News by a reader referred to "the workforce crisis posed by the Millennial generation." The screed noted how the generation is "illiterate and distracted," and will never reach maturity because their parents are their enablers, even to the extent of supporting "their every...unplanned pregnancy."[42]

Whoa. No wonder they chose to submit the letter anonymously. Thankfully the article's author pointed out the hypocrisy that exists among many generations that come before others: "Let's remember that older generations have always freaked out about the next few. And yet, here we are."[43]

Let's take a look at one of the facts behind our over-entitled narcisissm. In 2012, MTV's Research division (I didn't know they had such a thing, either) published the results of a study they conducted on Millennials' attitudes in the workplace. Eighty percent of the respondents indicated that they "want regular feedback from their boss."[44] While this seems straightforward, the difference in interpretation of this simple statement has been profound.

Forbes chose to go the way of the haters, entitling their article "Gimme Gimme Gimme – Millennials In the Workplace," and deriding the generation as needing "almost constant feedback." In a further demonstration of the intended tone, the article later went on to dismiss the survey's assertion that money was not a key motivator for the group with "My BS-o-meter gives this one a sideways glance."[45] If we aren't going to take the topic seriously then the analysis isn't worth the digital paper it's printed on.

The study was clear to mention that waiting for reviews on a six-month cycle was not in line with Millennials' expectations,[46] but thought

---

[42] Johnson, S. (2014, September 30). Ask Stacy: The Millennials Are Ruining This Country. What Can We Do? Retrieved August 26, 2015, from http://www.moneytalksnews.com/ask-stacy-1028-the-millennials-are-ruining-this-country-what-can-we-do/

[43] Ibid.

[44] Hillhouse, A. (2012, October 12). Consumer Insights: MTV's 'No Collar Workers' Retrieved August 26, 2015, from http://blog.viacom.com/2012/10/consumer-insights-mtvs-no-collar-workers/

[45] Kiisel, T. (2012, May 16). Gimme, Gimme, Gimme - Millennials In the Workplace. Retrieved August 26, 2015, from http://www.forbes.com/sites/tykiisel/2012/05/16/gimme-gimme-gimme-millennials-in-the-workplace/

[46] Schawbel, D. (2012, March 29). Millennials vs. Baby Boomers: Who Would You

leaders in the industry back that statement up as well. The Harvard Business Review recommends that supervisors "Practice giving feedback often; soon it will become a habit."[47] Good feedback should be given regularly, even as frequently as once per week or more.[48] I have given the same advice in my meetings with managers and business owners. If you're having a minor meltdown thinking of how you'd possibly fit in that many meetings, you can breathe a sigh of relief. Feedback and recognition can, and should, be informal and frequent to be effective. A simple thank you at the end of a tough day can be a big boost for a tired worker. If someone did a good job on a task or a project, it costs no money and practically no time to say 'great work.' On the converse, if someone is missing the mark, don't wait to tell them. Employees will often make corrections right away if told in a timely fashion, but feedback that waits six months loses most of its impact. If I've said it once, I've said it dozens of times: a performance review should not contain surprises.

This is something that doesn't just support a company's relationships with its younger workers – it's good for everyone. Towers Watson reports that companies where employees receive regular feedback and recognition from managers have more highly engaged workforces,[49] and engagement drives not only employee retention, but also lowers absenteeism, even boosts a company's profitability.[50]

Rather Hire? Retrieved August 26, 2015, from http://business.time.com/2012/03/29/millennials-vs-baby-boomers-who-would-you-rather-hire/

[47] Phoel, C. (2009, April 27). Feedback That Works. Retrieved October 26, 2015, from https://hbr.org/2009/04/feedback-that-works/

[48] Conrad, S. (2011, May 16). 5 Steps to Effective Employee Feedback. Retrieved August 26, 2015, from http://www.thedailymba.com/2011/05/16/5-steps-to-effective-employee-feedback/

[49] Towers Watson. (2009). *Turbocharging Employee Engagement: The Power of Recognition from Managers.* Retrieved August 26, 2015 from http://www.towerswatson.com/en/Insights/IC-Types/Ad-hoc-Point-of-View/Perspectives/2010/Perspectives-Turbocharging-Employee-Engagement

[50] Moreland, J. (2013, May 1). The Costs Of Ignoring Employee Engagement. Retrieved August 26, 2015, from http://www.fastcompany.com/3009012/the-costs-of-ignoring-employee-engagement

I think we can agree that frequent feedback is not just a Millennial trend, but if these facts weren't enough to convince you, allow me to tell you a story about my father.

Dad, a textbook Traditionalist, spent his career as a plumber. He worked on a number of major construction sites, and as we would drive around northern New Jersey, he would point to some of its best-known landmarks and say, "I put the toilets in that building." He was a talented worker, and in his later career worked as a site foreman and the president of his local. He loved his job, and he did it with no need for special praise.

I asked Dad one day if he had ever been recognized at work, and he told me about a week in his work life, many years ago. He was working at a local hospital replacing a huge industrial-sized boiler, as the supervisor of the job. His boss gave him a journeyman and an apprentice for the task, and five days to complete it. Dad took a look at the work, and as they began he realized the work could be done in only one day. Once completed, he reported back, and his manager was floored. A pat on the back and a couple of hundred dollars later, my parents were speeding down the Garden State Parkway to enjoy a weekend in Atlantic City, boss' treat.

Any business owner, especially one in similar trades, realizes why what my father did was significant. The hourly rates for these three workers, combined with the time they weren't spending doing other work, could amount to thousands of dollars. A couple of hundred dollars for a worker to go away for the weekend was just a small portion of what he saved the business.

A Traditionalist, however, doesn't work for recognition, and Dad said as much, when I asked what he thought of the gesture. "I didn't need him to do that for me. I would have done it anyway; I didn't need five days to do the job." I then asked if it changed how he felt about his job.

He summed it up in one sentence. "I would have bent over backwards for that man."

Imagine if all of your workers felt that way. Now take a moment and think about Millennials – they *want* to feel this way about work *all the time*.

Let's return to the MTV survey for a moment. I think they said it best, so I will quote them directly: "The quest for work that is "meaningful" and "makes a difference" has become a core Millennial trait. It's not "career pickiness," but an expression of a need to connect deeply with the work."[51] Perhaps it is unsurprising, then, that members of this generation make up the quickest-growing group of entrants to Seminaries in the United States. As noted by Rev. Thomas Baima in an interview with NPR, "It seems the Millennials are very much interested in lives of meaning and purpose, they want to do things that have some significance."[52]

Our task now is to figure out how to trigger that feeling in younger workers to not only attract them to work at your business, but encourage them to stay once they get there, and the first place I recommend business owners and senior leaders look is in their own hearts. Why did you get into this field in the first place? Why do you believe so strongly in this company that you are willing to spend upwards of sixty to eighty hours per week putting your best into it? What made you choose this, and not a different workplace or profession? This is what your young workers want to hear. Get personal – you want the job to feel personal to them, too.

Many companies have mission statements, but if challenged to recite it, workers often wouldn't know it. Other companies have no mission statement at all. It's hard to know whether a weak statement is worse than no statement, but in either situation it must be resolved. This is not an easy task, I will warn you. It is enough of a challenge to ask a

[51] Hillhouse, A. (2012, October 12). Consumer Insights: MTV's 'No Collar Workers' Retrieved August 26, 2015, from http://blog.viacom.com/2012/10/consumer-insights-mtvs-no-collar-workers/
[52] Pao, M. (2015, September 23). At U.S. Seminaries, A Rise In Millennials Answering God's Call. Retrieved September 29, 2015.

group to come up with where to order lunch, and the more passionate the group, the longer the discussion. Don't assume that you will sit down with your leadership team and come out with a cohesive statement an hour later. Let it be something that your team is allowed to think about over a period of time.

When launching the project, start small. Allow the group to brainstorm words or short phrases that they would like to suggest for inclusion. Once you've got a good start, piece those bits together. If the need arises, don't shy away from throwing the entire draft away to start fresh. This mission should be the call to action for your workers, and it should feel more like a Braveheart moment, and less like Waiting for Godot. Take your time and make it phenomenal.

Once you've devised your statement, a vision is an excellent follow-up. After you've won the hearts and minds of your employees, and they understand that working at your company is a great choice, you need to let them know where the company is going. Wherever possible, put tangible goals and numbers into the vision, because you are going to roll this out to your team and rally everyone together to make it happen. If it can be tracked in a visible way, such as a gauge on your company's website or a poster in the cafeteria, show your progress. Hold town hall meetings and share the results. Help everyone feel that they play a part in making these goals happen, and they will return the favor by driving your results. I'd be willing to wager it will work on someone from any generation.

Remember in the previous chapter when I talked about having the performance conversation with Millennials? Don't worry, I didn't forget. Inherent in the conversation about the company's goals, and how the individual creates those results, is where there is room for improvement, both in soft and hard skills.

Once you've shared the company's goals with the workforce, they should not merely sit there, awaiting fulfillment. They should be driven down the infrastructure, through managers to their individual reports. At the beginning of your performance management cycle, create the goals for each worker that will bear fruit for the company. Each position has a role to play, so set meaningful, challenging, but achievable marks for the year. Managers should discuss them with each employee, and the employee should be given the opportunity to talk about what they feel they need to achieve them. Invest in the trainings that will create results in a measured, thoughtful way.

Throughout the year, check back on these goals. Are they still achievable? Did the needs of the business change, shifting the team's priorities? If the employee is missing the mark, say so now, and figure out how to sharpen his or her skills so that they can reach their goals. At the end of the year, a review and wrap up of the work that was done should be the capstone on a year of work, improvement and achievement.

This process truly separates the wheat from the chaff. I've seen managers hesitate to challenge their workers, noting that it is struggle enough to get someone to do what they already have on their plates. If this is the case, ask yourself whether this person is in the right role for their abilities. Alternatively, perhaps the expectations of that person are misaligned. Empower yourself. Make the difficult decision to take action when needed. No one is helped by staying in a job that is less than appropriate for them.

The change in the nature of performance reviews from years ago is noticeable for older generations. Some workers will remember a time when reviews weren't done at all. The working world in general started a palpable change from an entitlement-driven culture to one that is more performance based, and it has had significant implications for not only how business is done, but the limits of what companies can accomplish.

Entitlement refers to earning your place, promotion or raise through putting in your time. The person who has been in a position the longest tends to have the most seniority, and tends to be considered first for incentives. If a position in management becomes available, it would go to the person with the most time on the job. This is still seen in union shops, where collective bargaining agreements are written to ensure this tradition remains alive. The weakness in this system is that there may be a more talented person behind who has less time on the job, but would be far more valuable from the business' perspective.

Another challenge in an entitlement culture is the incentives. If what gets you to the next rung on the ladder is being in the job longest, risk taking is not advisable. Keep your head down, don't challenge the status quo, and make differences in little ways. If you take a big chance and try to make waves, you may lose your job, and all your prospects with it. You'll start over again somewhere else. But in organizations where risks aren't taken, the biggest gains are not realized. To me, a perfect example of this philosophy is Elon Musk. The co-founder of PayPal made a name for himself in business, but became a famous figure for his riskiest ventures: SpaceX, Tesla and the Hyperloop. He had to borrow a lot of money from banks and even his own personal circle of friends to go from great to legendary, and on that he said, "If something is important enough, even if the odds are against you, you should still do it."[53]

Work culture has now taken on a much more performance-driven atmosphere. Individuals' performance is being studied for strengths and weaknesses as companies build their bench of capable workers. Leaders can plan how knowledge and experience will affect long-term workflow, and planning is the rule of the game. Workers can be deployed exactly where they will have the most impact, and can be developed to bring greater value as their careers progress. The entitlement culture had an increasingly difficult time competing against companies with that type of human capital strategy.

Having not grown up in a world where entitlement culture was as valuable, it was easy to see why we would not feel bound to it. We don't feel that people earn career progression through time, but through ability.

---

[53] Hibbard, S. (2012, October 15). 5 Lessons from Big Idea Guy, Elon Musk. Retrieved October 26, 2015, from http://www.themarketingbit.com/marketing-lessons/marketing-5-lessons-from-big-idea-guy-elon-musk-infographic/

I'm willing to bet that a fair number of us, no matter the generation, have seen a promotion go to someone that should have really belonged to someone else, but because of a silly rule both the employee and the company got less than they deserve. Pair this experience with the passion a Millennial feels for the job, and you can understand why we wouldn't hesitate to walk into the CEO's office during our first week on the job. We're not just here to work, we're here to absolutely crush it for ourselves, our bosses and the team.

You may be a bit bemused at this point, because you've heard so much about how Generation Y is lazy, doesn't work hard, and just doesn't have the work ethic of other generations. It's tough to square this myth with what we've just discussed, so it's time to put it to rest.

Myth #3: Millennials Are Unmotivated

"They are lazy, entitled narcissists." – Joel Stein, Time Magazine

I'm going to just come out and say it – unmotivated is just another word for lazy, and I have heard it plenty of times. Recently, during a conversation with a couple of family members, it came up without reservation. It was used to describe the checkout staff at the supermarket, who, unlike his forebears of fifty years ago, couldn't be bothered to put in the extra effort into making the experience quick, pleasant and memorable. "Your generation is lazy," they said, exasperated.

Of course, if challenged to answer whether that meant I was also lazy, they would rush to say that I was not. I had a full time job that required a lot of effort, I was writing a book (that they weren't aware they would be quoted in at the time), I had a toddler and a husband and we were buying a house. The logical conclusion, then, is that I must be the only member of my generation who isn't lazy. The weight of an entire generation's achievements rests on my very tired shoulders.

Other Millennials have faced this same fallacy. The whole generation is unmotivated, save for the numerous grandchildren, nieces, nephews and well-mannered neighbors who were the lone exceptions. I'm sad to say that we even say it about ourselves, and each other. A Pew Research Center study demonstrated that this generation doesn't want to be called 'Millennial', and disassociates themselves from a group that has gotten such a bad reputation, one that doesn't represent them in the least.[54] Like many reputations, however, it is undeserved, and has spread like a nasty rumor at a homecoming dance.

I think it's time we put this one to rest with one very simple truth: you can divide a population into groups by nearly any measure – race, gender, age, nationality, random sample, etc. – and find a group of lazy people among them. Further, those unmotivated individuals would tend to self-select into jobs that didn't require 60-hour work weeks, advanced degrees or a high degree of self-regulation. A supermarket job has a low barrier to entry for these individuals. That, however, is too easy a conclusion, and I don't want to dismiss the discussion so quickly.

Rather than laziness, I think a loss of prestige better explains the change in the grocery store experience, and many other retail roles. There seems to be a decline of the pride that people take in jobs like these, and I would assert part of the reason for this is due to two factors: low wages and the high cost of exceptional customer service.

In your typical chain supermarket, the median annual income a cashier can expect to make is $28,444.[55] This is just slightly higher than the federal poverty level for a family of four. As I mentioned previously, money is a hygiene factor, and while pay that is too high can lead to diminishing returns, pay that is too low results in poor engagement and low motivation. It's tough to go the extra mile when you don't make enough to make ends meet, and stress is well known to erode productivity. Compare this to the 1970's, when that era's minimum wage went much farther than it does today.[56] You could actually make a living working at a grocer, and the position was treated as such by the

---

[54] Basu, T. (2015, September 3). Millennials Don't Like to Call Themselves Millennials. Retrieved October 26, 2015, from http://time.com/4021479/millennial-generation-pew/

[55] Cashier - Grocery Store Salary (n.d.). Retrieved September 24, 2015, from http://www1.salary.com/Cashier-Grocery-Store-Salary.html

[56] DeSilver, D. (2014, September 8). Who makes minimum wage? Retrieved September 24, 2015, from http://www.pewresearch.org/fact-tank/2014/09/08/who-makes-minimum-wage/

management as well. It wasn't a job where people would automatically look down their nose at you simply for wearing a nametag, as I myself experienced while working at a supermarket, and others surely do in similar occupations. The life of a typical cashier has changed dramatically.

There are, however, grocery stores where the experience is very different, and the example I often use is Trader Joe's. At Trader Joe's, I'm most often greeted by a smiling cashier who makes polite chit-chat, quickly and accurately rings up my order, bags it so my sprouted-grain bread doesn't get squashed under my fair-trade coffee, and sees me out with commendable efficiency. The entire store has a pleasant shopping atmosphere, including corny but adorable decorations, tastings of their products, and high-quality, healthy food choices (and some naughty ones). This is surely the supermarket experience that my family was mourning the loss of, but it's not an accident or a fluke. Cashiers at Trader Joe's earn an average salary of $40,000 per year – *to start.*[57] The wages only go up with tenure. An associate said it plainly: "They pay enough to keep employees happy." Combine that with family-friendly scheduling and an attractive benefit package and you have a recipe for success.[58]

The typical rejoinder to this argument is that these jobs aren't meant for working parents or mid-career workers, but rather for young people to earn some extra cash while they are in school. They seem to conveniently forget when that wasn't the case. We've slowly relegated jobs like these into a category that makes it less than what we'd expect from an adult supporting a family, and then wonder why we're not getting the same customer-is-always-right treatment.

Whether or not these jobs are now only intended as side gigs, it is not turning out to be the practice. Workers ages sixteen to twenty-four are only a slight majority of minimum wage earners.[59] As the economy

---

[57] Quinton, S. (2013, March 25). The Trader Joe's Lesson: How to Pay a Living Wage and Still Make Money in Retail. Retrieved September 24, 2015.
[58] For Cashier, the Deal is A-OK at Trader Joe's. (2013, July 24). Retrieved September 24, 2015, from http://womensenews.org/story/labor/130722/cashier-the-deal-ok-at-trader-joes

recovers and more jobs open, this may change, but especially during the Great Recession, people went where the jobs were, and that was often low wage retail and fast food positions. Our feelings on whether or not workers belong in the jobs they have will have no effect on their morale if their treatment in those jobs is not commensurate with what they need to survive in an increasingly expensive, stressful world.

Another contributing factor to both low-energy associates and low productivity is the second-job phenomenon. For students who are giving their all to earning a degree, that part time job is only their side hustle. Many minimum wage workers also turn to second jobs to make ends meet – five percent of the American workforce has two or more jobs.[60] At some point a person's willpower and energy will wane, so that spaced-out teenager behind the counter may actually be a straight-A student who studied with a tutor, attended all her classes and wrote a paper before coming to work, and she just doesn't have much left to spend more time or effort than exactly as much as it will take to keep her job.

I alluded earlier to the high cost of customer service, and I can think of no better example of this than Best Buy. In an economy where the value of the bargain trumps nearly everything for the consumer, the big box electronics retailer has managed to drive prices lower and lower. In order to do so, costs must be cut elsewhere, and one way to do so is to replace knowledgeable experts with low-wage workers. If you walk into one of their stores and ask the nearest associate for advice on which DSLR camera to buy, they will often simply check the product information tags on the shelf for differences and report them back to you. On the other hand, stores that still trade in the old-fashioned way of comparison shopping, such as J&R, offer products at a higher price point, but behind

[59] Noah, T. (2014, May 23). The average minimum wage worker today is not who you think. Retrieved September 24, 2015, from http://www.msnbc.com/msnbc/average-minimum-wage-worker-myth
[60] Sauter, A., Hess, A., & Frohlich, T. (2014, January 21). States where the most people work two jobs. Retrieved September 24, 2015.

the counter is someone who can tell you the differences between products without having to consult a cheat sheet. People with this type of knowledge and experience won't be attracted to minimum wage jobs, so it will cost more for a company to employ them. Unfortunately, due to low-price competitors and online price-slashers like Amazon, that customer service model is being threatened because the traditional way of doing things can't compete.

One of the most often cited facts about Millennials that are used to prop up the myth of our laziness is that we still live with our parents. The facts reveal that as many as a third of the members of this generation are still living in multi-generational family households.[61] And why not, especially if they don't have to contribute to household expenses, cook for themselves or do their own laundry. It's a lazy person's dream.

We can dispense with the notion of laziness on the part of this generation, then, because many are reporting that they do not wish to continue living with their parents, but feel that it is the best choice for them at this time.[62] The trend began because of the crippling economic prospects facing them upon graduation, but even as the job market improves, Generation Y isn't moving out yet.[63] The cost of housing coupled with extremely strict lending standards may be partially to blame.

In 2015, we're seeing a problem of supply and demand. The availability of homes for purchase is far lower than the demand (we all

---

[61] Fry, R. (2015, July 29). More Millennials Living With Family Despite Improved Job Market. Retrieved September 24, 2015, from http://www.pewsocialtrends.org/2015/07/29/more-millennials-living-with-family-despite-improved-job-market/

[62] Tuttle, B. (2012, November 8). Millennials: Turns Out the 'Entitled Generation' Is Willing to Sacrifice. Retrieved September 24, 2015, from http://business.time.com/2012/11/08/millennials-turns-out-the-entitled-generation-is-willing-to-sacrifice/

[63] Fry, R. (2015, July 29). More Millennials Living With Family Despite Improved Job Market. Retrieved September 24, 2015, from http://www.pewsocialtrends.org/2015/07/29/more-millennials-living-with-family-despite-improved-job-market/

want to move out of our parents' homes, you see), and it has driven prices sky high. The median home price is now $228,700, compared to $76,400 in 1980, according to the Census Bureau. In thirty-five years the average home price has nearly tripled. I don't think I need to tell you that our wages haven't. Thanks to the prevalence of bad mortgage lending prior to the financial crisis of 2008, many people were able to buy homes, even with no money down, whereas today's reactionary standards would not allow for that (nor should they). Despite mortgage rates at record lows, it's difficult to take advantage of the situation.

With all these facts considered, perhaps you can sympathize with us when we get angry at our inability to do the very same things our parents did at our age being blamed on our perceived laziness. "Millennials say they're smart with their cash. They're not. Over half admit they're 'living paycheck to paycheck'," writes Ben Shapiro on Breitbart.com. "More than one in three still draw cash or resources from mom and dad."[64] It hurts even more that he himself is a Millennial, but he's also among our many well-known crazies.

So, to summarize, claims about our laziness are exaggerated and overgeneralized. Your goal is to not pay too little, and not pay too much. Especially as our economy tilts away from an employer's dream to an employee's marketplace, attracting workers with the right package for your business is critical. It begins before the vacancy even becomes available, with devising a pay strategy that will support the current aims of the company, as well as future plans. Many business owners that I've spoken to will say that they have waited until a critical position was open to begin recruiting, and in the rush to find a suitable replacement before business is lost, they've paid dearly to meet the right employee's salary parameters, almost as if the company was held hostage and needed to meet this person's demands, with their clients' service being held in the balance.

---

[64] Shapiro, B. (2015, February 3). 7 Reasons Millennials Are The Worst Generation. Retrieved October 25, 2015, from http://www.breitbart.com/big-government/2015/02/03/7-reasons-millennials-are-the-worst-generation/

In order to devise an appropriate pay strategy, research must be done in what the market is currently paying for your role, as well as what position your company will take in that market. Being the company that pays the most is not feasible for anyone but that top-paying business, so strategize your pay around the other aspects of your offer package. Not-for-profits, for example, have traditionally offered a stronger benefits package to offset lower salaries, although this will surely change as healthcare costs do. Perhaps your company serves a high-end clientele – a market-leading pay strategy will share profits with your workers, but also contribute to a high-end experience for them, which can be reflected in the service experience. If your business is bigger on heart than profits, your compensation strategy should reflect that – but be sure your recruiting headline is the great work you do, and the sense of community and togetherness the culture has (and make sure it does – but we'll get to that later).

Once you've decided on your strategy and you have some hard numbers to back it, make sure you implement and enforce it. When it comes time for merit raises, check where your employees are in the pay range, and reward based on that data, as well as their performance. If your merit raises are little more than a cost of living increase, then don't call it merit. We all know what you really mean, and we aren't feeling rewarded by it.

Critically, when it comes time to recruit for that unicorn candidate who will fill the vacancy expertly and mesh perfectly with your culture, stick to your compensation guns. It's tempting to just pay whatever they've asked for because you desperately want that individual on your team so badly, but if it's the right fit, the money will only be one of many factors. Introduce that person to members of the team, show them the great work your company does, and talk about the corporate social responsibility agenda. They will be the right fit regardless of whether they can be paid more elsewhere, as long as the pay at your job is fair.

It would be difficult at this point to not mention some of the crazy-high compensation that some executives in our country are paid. I don't think I'll be the first person to say that there is a pretty stark difference between some of the most highly-paid workers in the United States and the average worker. I'm not an economist, but Robert Reich agrees, and asserts that it's a drag on the overall health of the nation's financial picture, as well as that of individuals.[65] We've all been watching as this new type of soap opera plays out on the news, and it leaves a bad taste in most people's mouths.

What Millennials want is not the executives' paychecks, but to be on the same team. We value a collaborative, team approach to work, and transparency is a big part of that.[66] If we're struggling to move out of our tiny apartment, and we've delayed having children because of it (and this is happening more and more frequently[67]), it's hard to feel like we're all pulling together when the top member of our organization makes ten times what we do. It's even harder when the actual fact is that the top CEOs in our country make *three hundred times* what the average worker in their organizations do.[68] Much of that compensation data is public knowledge. Rest assured we are looking, and rest equally assured that it's creating a feeling of resentment and disengagement in companies where this fact is a brutal reality.

I think this trend will eventually change as Millennials rise through the ranks, if our values hold out (and I sincerely hope they do). When

_____

[65] Reich, R. (2014, September 28). Why the Economy is Still Failing Most Americans. Retrieved October 13, 2015, from http://robertreich.org/post/98668011635
[66] Sellers, P. (2015, July 15). Millennials want this one thing from employers. Retrieved October 13, 2015.
[67] Cox, J. (2015, May 4). Bad news for older folks: Millennials are having fewer babies. Retrieved October 13, 2015, from https://www.washingtonpost.com/opinions/among-millennials-theres-a-baby-bust/2015/05/04/c98d5a08-f295-11e4-84a6-6d7c67c50db0_story.html
[68] Mischel, L., & Davis, A. (2015, June 21). Top CEOs Make 300 Times More than Typical Workers: Pay Growth Surpasses Stock Gains and Wage Growth of Top 0.1 Percent. Retrieved October 13, 2015, from http://www.epi.org/publication/top-ceos-make-300-times-more-than-workers-pay-growth-surpasses-market-gains-and-the-rest-of-the-0-1-percent/

surveyed about their leadership aspirations, forty-three percent of respondents of this generation responded their biggest motivation in achieving top positions in their field was to empower others. Those that were motivated primarily by money only comprised five percent of respondents.[69] I genuinely felt good when first learned that statistic, because I've seen plenty of people with the most virtuous intentions sell out completely when they finally got to the top, and it galled me. We won't be like that, I've always said to myself. Let's make sure we aren't, friends. A lot of eyes are on us.

But we've still got some growing to do before we get there, so let's focus on the present.

Like any worker, when properly motivated, Millennials will be a thriving part of your workforce, but each generation, and indeed people in general, are all motivated differently. For some reason, though, the things that motivated the generations before us are considered acceptable, whereas our generation is being dismissed as greedy, our demands outlandish. If challenged to name what are the things we look for in a job, however, many are hard-pressed to actually describe these factors. Let's unpack that now.

---

[69] Buss, D. (2015, July 30). 6 Insights: What Kind of Leaders Millennials Will Be. Retrieved October 13, 2015, from http://chiefexecutive.net/6-insights-into-what-kind-of-leaders-millennials-will-be/

Myth #4: Millennials Are Ungrateful

Try to remember back to a birthday when you were a child when your grandmother (or Aunt Gertie, or some other elder woman in your life) bestowed upon you a heartfelt gift. For some it was the incredibly scratchy sweater she knit by hand; for others it was an action figure that, while super cool, was just a small part of a much bigger toy set that you didn't own. You looked down at the gift and realized you needed to craft a reaction that would convince both grandma and your watchful mother that you loved it, and you were grateful. Failure to show gratitude was not just rudeness on your part, but also a perceived reflection on your own longsuffering mom, who would be mortified if anyone thought for a second that she had raised an ungrateful little brat.

This is the situation many Millennials find themselves in, but instead of grandma it's the workplace, and instead of your stern mother it's the older generations, watching down on us, hoping that we don't embarrass them by being petulant little fools. It seems that we may not have measured up in this regard, because there is a lot of tsk-tsk-ing going on regarding our seeming inability to just accept what we've been handed and manage to put a smile on our face.

Both in the micro and macro versions of these situations, we've hit upon one of humanity's more delicate conundrums: the idea that the receiver of a gift, no matter how impractical, inappropriate or unwanted, should be met with unadulterated thanksgiving. It strikes at the inherent selfishness of giving, that while we want to give of ourselves to others and say we want nothing in return for it, we actually do want something in return. We want the ego stroke.

Mind you, not everyone is the same way. After all, plenty of anonymous donors exist solely to give of themselves and see the world improve. However, most humans want to see that their altruism is met with an appropriate level of acknowledgement. Otherwise, there would be no "I Gave Blood" stickers, park benches named for givers, or gifts with donations (although I do have my eye on that NPR tote bag). We shouldn't push this away as a knee-jerk reflex – it's okay to want to be recognized for doing good things. Plenty of charitable organizations host awards to honor the selfless among their ranks. It inspires others to do good and it makes you feel good for doing it. Don't waste time rejecting this notion just so you don't have to feel guilty about it.

So when we get the scratchy sweater, we flash a smile at our auntie and thank her for putting her time and effort into something that reflected her love for us. Do we wear it? Absolutely not. Well, maybe the next time she comes over, but certainly not to school or anything.

This, to me, is a fair metaphor for Millennials in the workplace. When we find ourselves on the hunt for a job, we go looking with hope that someone will recognize the good in us and find it in their hearts to offer us a job. When that job turns out to be less than a great fit, or the culture in the workplace is broken, or when we don't get a decent work-life balance out of it, the gratitude is hollow. We'll take the position, we'll thank you for giving us the chance, and we'll wear it when you come over, but as soon as you're not looking at us we'll be on the hunt for a much more comfortable role.

Let's extend the metaphor even further. That sweater you got as a gift was given with all of the best intentions. After all, grandma comes from a time when clothes were not as commodified as they are now. It wasn't as easy to just go out and buy a new one. Money was tight, and it was made to last far longer than our clothes do now. There wasn't much buying "this season's" fashions, because it was impractical. So when she sits down and thinks about what she's going to give you for your birthday, she thinks that she is going to give of her time and energy to find the perfect yarn for you and painstakingly knit it into a useful object that will last you a long time. Arthritis is no joke, you know.

I believe this is what might be happening on the part of Traditionalist and Baby Boomer recruiters and business leaders. They have a position, you need a paycheck. If you can be matched with that situation you should be glad you have a job, because there are plenty of people who are unemployed or underemployed out there, and you have just been rescued from another month of eating cat food so you can pay your rent. Whereas this may have been true for those generations, it's not the case anymore.

Once they upgrade from cat food, Generation Y is not simply satisfied by having a job. We consider a job to be a two-way street. If you employ us, you will be paying me for my work. However, we don't expect to have to sacrifice spending time with our children to satisfy the needs of the position. Take care of us, and we'll take care of you. If we bring lots of new business to the company, accomplish great things and help raise the stock price, we expect that you'll similarly help us raise our own stock price, be it in social, familial or financial capital.

It's not solely about family time, either. For those of us without children, we shouldn't have to give up Saturday nights with our buddies at the bar to finish up our reports each week. This, by the way, is a huge sticking point for us – it shouldn't only be people with kids at home that get to reap the pleasures of work-life balance benefits. We hate hearing that we should be the ones to work on holidays because we don't have kids. It's as if we won't matter until we hit that milestone. Perhaps we have a darling older loved one who hosts the holiday, and we don't have unlimited opportunities to spend time with her for the rest of our lives. And yes, we're wearing that sweater she knit us; it will make her so happy. Even worse, many Millennials have had to delay having children because their incomes in the very jobs that promise us eventual work-life balance don't support them moving out, buying a home and starting that family. We've noted the irony, and we're not amused.

This brings me to the crux of my argument: simply giving a gift is insufficient to expect gratitude in return. The gift has to be something that we'll like, something that pairs with an interest we hold, or something that will help us accomplish a goal. I'm reminded of a gift from my mother, given for my birthday that helped me raise money to teach English in Guatemala. As she gave it to me, she said, "I'm helping you, but I don't want you to do this anymore." She recognized that Central America can be a dangerous place, and a young woman travelling alone faces enhanced dangers. But at the end of the day, she knew the cardinal rule of gift giving: bring joy to the receiver, not yourself.

Knowing this, there are two ways to look at hiring Millennials. You can dig your heels in, say that we're ungrateful, that we should just be happy to get a job, and continue to be frustrated at how hard it is to find good workers and keep them. Alternatively, you can recognize that your feelings in the situation don't matter at all, and in order to attract and retain the best workers, you're going to need to make it worth their while, not yours.

This does not mean, however, that you should throw every perk and reward you can afford at your workers in order to keep up with the Joneses. Or rather, to keep up with the Googles. This is a canard many point to when bemoaning the ridiculous expectations Millennials have at the workplace. Three meals a day cooked by a world-class chef, on-site car washes and dry cleaning and all the snacks you can pack in, all for free, just to bring in the best and brightest the young workforce has to offer. What many don't realize, however, is that this comes at a price. Google isn't offering all of those things so you take the job, they are offering them so you won't leave once you get to the office in the morning. No more rushing off-campus to get your chores done if you can just do them at work. Hunger won't be that final thing that pushes you to shut down and head home for the evening if you have unlimited food at your disposal. There are expectations that come with all those perks, and Googlers work hard. There are a lot of sacrifices for that, however, which may explain why in 2013 the average tenure of a worker at that company was just a little over a year.[70]

We don't want to wait until we retire to begin getting the most out of life. We want to be able to enjoy the entire time, so work-life balance is critical for our job satisfaction and is a key or primary factor for this generation in their job search.[71] If you aren't yet comfortable with a workplace that rejects the strict 9-to-5 regime, you will be happy to learn that it does not automatically equate to a loss of productivity, nor will it impact your ability to manage your team.

The first thing you should realize is that there are very few jobs nowadays that require a worker to be at a desk during particular hours. Think about it: laptops are cheaper than desktops, allow for portability, and with VPN networks, a worker can do the same work at their desk as in a park, on the beach, or at home. If the worker isn't working directly with the public, using special machinery or providing security to an area, requiring them to sit at a desk is a reflex of managerial style, company culture or mere tradition. Even team collaboration can be done virtually, thanks to internet meeting rooms, webcams and file-sharing and collaboration software.

Divorce yourself now from the idea that the age-old cubicle is the best way to make sure work gets done. In fact, more and more studies have shown that remote workers are actually more productive that those who are required to be in the workplace.[72] Think about it: there are a lot

---

[70] Giang, V. (2013, July 28). Ranking America's Biggest Companies By Turnover Rate. Retrieved October 24, 2015, from http://www.slate.com/blogs/business_insider/2013/07/28/turnover_rates_by_company_how_amazon_google_and_others_stack_up.html

[71] Cox, J. (2015, May 5). Millennials want a work-life balance. Their bosses just don't get why. Retrieved October 24, 2015, from https://www.washingtonpost.com/local/millennials-want-a-work-life-balance-their-bosses-just-dont-get-why/2015/05/05/1859369e-f376-11e4-84a6-6d7c67c50db0_story.html

[72] Desmarais, C. (2014, January 30). More Evidence It's a Mistake to Make

of things that impede work flow in the office. Birthday cake. Fire drills. Lookie-loos passing by your desk. None of those things exist at home. Employees who work at home can control their environment much more, so all of the things that would cause them a distraction can be eliminated or dealt with. Further, you won't have to wait until your strangely loud cube mate gets off the phone so you can reach out to that client.

Sure, you may be saying, but how will I know they are actually working? Let me disabuse you now of the notion that you can measure how much a person is working by periodically glancing at them or walking by. Actual productivity is measured in number of calls, meeting deadlines or other metrics, not by observation. If that's the only method you're currently using, you are missing a big opportunity to actually understand what your workers get done. Not to mention, there is plenty of procrastination happening at work, which is why websites and social media feeds have learned to append some of their more blue content with the NSFW tag – Not Safe For Work. It's happening around you when you are not looking, and even sometimes when you are. There are websites that provide official-looking spreadsheet graphics for a worker to click to quickly when you are near so it appears that they are working. One even replicates Twitter in Excel format.

Shame on you if you aren't already measuring your worker's output in a more effective way. Once you start, though, you can begin to loosen the reins a bit and let someone catch up on that project during the evening so they can catch their son's starring role as a mushroom in the local production of Stone Soup. And sure, let your childless worker come in late so he can surprise his girlfriend with brunch. He'll be grateful for it, and he'll make up the work.

Don't believe me? Let's say he never does make up the work and he misses a deadline. This is where your counseling and discipline

Employees Work in the Office. Retrieved October 24, 2015, from http://www.inc.com/christina-desmarais/want-productive-employees-let-some-of-them-work-from-home.html processes come in, so it's not like he's running roughshod over you. Moreover, it's far better that you both plan for his absence in advance than he calls out 'sick' and you're left holding the bag. Work-life balance improves absenteeism.[73]

Keep in mind, you should be in control of the situation at all times. Set expectations early and often. Lay out time frames and deadlines when you assign work, well before anyone wants to take time off. Check in with your team during regular intervals so you can get a handle on how much work is being done and what is left. If you see the team heading toward disaster, you can take action well before it's too late.

Won't people take advantage, you may be asking? When no one is watching it's even easier to blow off work to look at cute cats on the internet (like the one below). If the only reason your workers get anything done is to avoid getting in trouble, you have a much bigger problem on your hands, and I'd be willing to bet a productivity drain as well. This reflects that your employees don't feel connected with what they are doing, or see the value in it. They don't clearly understand how what they are doing contributes to everyone's success. Go back and re-read chapter three.

---

[73] Chandler, A. (2015, July 28). How can employers and employees reduce workplace absenteeism and improve work/life balance? Retrieved October 24, 2015, from http://www.devonshire.co.uk/blogs/3/01f48n-how-can-employers-and-employees-reduce-workplace-absenteeism-and-improve-work/life-balance?

But, you may object in exasperation, even if all of this is true, won't it be harder to get my team feeling like a team? The camaraderie of a workplace is often a big cultural selling point. Working with great people is not only a recipe for the company's success, but it is something Millennials frequently point to as something they expect at work.[74] This is where all that time you used to spend walking around as a management tool can be put to much better use. Make plans! If a birthday is coming up for someone on your team, plan a lunch out for them. Did everyone just finish a huge project to massive acclaim? Take the time to celebrate with a party. If you want to double down on your management ROI, plan a volunteer event for the team to come together and accomplish something for a good cause. This will not only get everyone together and cooperating, but you can also check off social responsibility on your Millennial wish list.[75]

Let's return to our concept of giving. While it not only reflects on what makes a person happy in their job, there are also significant reasons to consider the giver-receiver conundrum when planning and executing on your recognition program. When you recognize your employees, make it something they'll truly respond to, not just in the material bit, but also in the presentation. You wouldn't want to congratulate the most shy, reserved person on your team by parading them in front of their peers at your next huddle to have them all shout and clap for him. He could be so mortified by the gesture that he'll never do another good thing again. Instead, write him a handwritten note and tuck a gift card for a cup of coffee at his favorite place inside.

---

[74] Giang, V. (2013, June 15). 71% Of Millennials Want Their Co-Workers To Be A 'Second Family' Retrieved October 24, 2015, from http://www.businessinsider.com/millennials-want-to-be-connected-to-their-coworkers-2013-6
[75] Cobb, M. (2014, July 7). Passion for a Cause: Millennials Want to Work and Volunteer Together | United Way Worldwide. Retrieved October 24, 2015, from http://www.unitedway.org/blog/passion-for-a-cause-millennials-want-to-work-and-volunteer-together

The gift you choose will have an impact as well. Let's say you have a worker on your team who you know loves hockey. One week, after she puts in a lot of time on a project and totally knocks it out of the park, you decide you want to show her how grateful you and the company are for her contributions, so you buy her tickets to the Devils game at the Prudential Center. You put them in a nice envelope, gather her co-workers around and make a big display of congratulating her. Everyone cheers, and you hand her the envelope. She looks up at you and smiles quietly, and returns to her desk.

Wait a minute – did she just give you the grandma sweater smile? That was hardly what you were expecting. How ungrateful! Meanwhile, she's selling the tickets on StubHub to buy the ones that she was really hoping would be in there, that of the greatest hockey team to ever take the ice, the New York Rangers. She's wondering how it could possibly be that you've been working together for as long as you have and you didn't know who her favorite team was. Recognition failed, motivation diminished.

Take your time and do recognition the right way. Big, expensive gestures will miss the mark if the gift means nothing to the recipient. Small gestures can go a long way when they are thoughtful and considered. If you really want to get an A-plus for your recognition program, make sure employees have a way of recognizing their peers, too.

All of these factors will go a long way to providing a workplace that Millennials will really feel grateful to be a part of, but these are just culture perks. Before we get to this point the rubber really has to meet the road when it comes to offering meaningful benefit packages, and in today's world it's getting harder and harder to do that. Let's take a look at what Millennials really want out of their offer letter next.

Go Rangers.

Myth #5: Millennials Want Everything

"Millennials can be surprisingly unaware of the inherent social contract most of us subscribe to, and tend to demonstrate a consistent and wide-eyed entitlement. They often lack even the most rudimentary sense of how to change themselves for the better. Millennials are noisy, narcissistic, and passive aggressive." – Stan Brown, What's Wrong With Millennials? 50 Things You Need to Know About the Entitled Generation

There was a time when people didn't feel that medical benefits were a necessity. Truly, medical care in general was not considered a necessity, because it lacked the scientific reliability that we expect today. You would get a poultice of some sort, rub it on the affected area, and hopefully whatever you had would go away. This wasn't really very long ago, in fact even in the early 20th century homeopathic remedies were how most people treated their illnesses and injuries.[76] Of course, back then you could only expect to live into your mid- to late-40s.[77]

Once health advances started to take off in the 1920's, all of a sudden people became more interested in receiving medical care, and doctors and hospitals became knowledge centers where people would go for whatever cures they needed. The first medical plan, so to speak, was offered around that time by a doctor who allowed a group of teachers to

---

[76] Blumberg, A., & Davidson, A. (2009, October 22). Accidents Of History Created U.S. Health System. Retrieved October 25, 2015, from http://www.npr.org/templates/story/story.php?storyId=114045132

[77] Life expectancy in the USA, 1900-98. (n.d.). Retrieved October 25, 2015, from http://demog.berkeley.edu/~andrew/1918/figure2.html

pay a monthly fee to receive treatment any time they wanted it. You may recognize the name it went by – Blue Cross.[78]

It wasn't until after World War II that health benefits started to be associated with job perks. Companies were under price controls, so salaries were not as negotiable. Enter the benefit package, a way to attract employees that was untaxed and valuable. That worked for a few decades, and many more employers followed suit, and perhaps because of all of the administrivia associated with multitudinous prices, packages, plans and providers, the costs skyrocketed.[79]

The picture of health benefits in our country is becoming murkier and harder to predict as we go forward with the implementation of the Affordable Care Act (ACA). It has faced its biggest and most compelling challenges and survived, so the effects of the law are coming upon us with greater speed and intensity. What used to be a somewhat predictable cost of doing business has now turned into a monster that many don't know how to deal with.

To begin with, the costs are out of control. The average premium for benefits has risen twenty-seven percent over the last five years,[80] and we are left wondering if there is even a ceiling. For the largest organizations the coping is a bit easier. With bigger employee pools the costs are easier to digest, but for small businesses that wish to compete, the barriers are sometimes insurmountable. I've spoken to business owners who understand the value of offering benefits to their employees, but even the bare minimum coverage is crippling for them, so their alternative is to offer nothing or even to take benefits away when they had been able to provide them previously, and they don't like that choice. Even companies that aren't required to meet the obligations under the

---

[78] Ibid.

[79] Emanuel, E., & Wyden, R. (2008, December 10). Why Tie Health Insurance to a Job? Retrieved October 25, 2015, from http://www.wsj.com/articles/SB122887085038593345

[80] EHBS 2015 – Summary Of Findings – 8775. (2015, September 22). Retrieved October 25, 2015.

ACA are squeezed, and their employees pushed out to the marketplace. It's no longer a given that a company can rely on benefits to attract employees.

What is the company to do? It depends on what you are capable of doing. I've counseled many business owners that offering a benefit to an employee is only going to be a gain for the business if the costs can be sustained and there is a tangible return on that investment, either in retention or employee engagement. It serves absolutely no one to cobble together a benefit package that is low on options and high on costs if practically no one participates in it. Crunch your numbers and see what you can afford, then see what that money will get you. If you can't offer a decent package, and you aren't obligated to, then don't bother.

If you are over the mark and required to comply with the provisions of the ACA, you need to decide whether to pay or play. Again, run your numbers and see what you can afford. If one of those options works into your budget and the other doesn't, your choice is easy. Your employees can go to the marketplace and find benefits, and with an increase in innovative health plan offerings, it will become easier and easier for employees to find a plan they like and buy it.

For example, in the New York area we have a company called Oscar, which offers health insurance and aims to target the hipster generation. It's goal is to offer simple solutions, technical options for accessing care, and a kinder, softer face than the intimidating monoliths that traditional companies have become. As the first company of its kind, it has been seen as a disrupter of the status quo,[81] so just as prior disrupters like Uber and TaskRabbit have been changing the face of services we've often taken as a given, Oscar could revolutionize how benefits are provided to the public. Its success could dictate how future competitors enter the market and operate within it. If your company

---

[81] Rosin, T. (2015, August 4). 10 things to know about Oscar Health Insurance: Will it be the Uber of health plans? Retrieved October 25, 2015, from http://www.beckershospitalreview.com/payer-issues/10-things-to-know-about-oscar-health-insurance-will-it-be-the-uber-of-health-plans.html

chooses to offer benefits, it would be worth it to take a page from Oscar, who now has a roster of 40,000 subscribers after its founding two years ago, and will shortly have expanded to cover California and Texas.[82]

It may not surprise you to learn that the generation that prizes customization and personalization would want their benefit plans to do the same thing. They want a choice in what kind of plans are offered so they can tailor their plan based on what they need and what they are willing to pay.[83] Provide a variety of supplemental plans that employees can elect, such as Catastrophic Illness or Personal Injury insurance. Oscar offers a selection of plans at different price points, rejecting the one size fits all approach. They also provide subscribers the opportunity to seek care outside of the doctor's office in places where it might be easier to do so, such as local pharmacies.[84] When having the conversation with your benefit broker, make sure that there are similar options available, and choose accordingly.

This generation also wants to be able to understand and control their choices while they use their plans,[85] much like we discussed with their 401(k)s. Make sure plan choices are explained thoroughly during open enrollment, and encourage questions. Bring in representatives from the healthcare provider who can help people explore their options. Demand superior customer service from your providers, and ensure that

[82] Tracer, Z. (2015, September 3). For Health Insurance Startup Oscar, Cute Ads Only Go So Far. Retrieved October 25, 2015, from http://www.bloomberg.com/news/articles/2015-09-03/for-health-insurance-startup-oscar-cute-ads-only-go-so-far

[83] Taurasi, L. (2015, June 3). 8 Great Employee Benefits Millennials Actually Want. Retrieved October 25, 2015, from http://workplace.care.com/8-great-employee-benefits-millennials-actually-want

[84] Fisher, N. (2013, August 19). Say Hi To Oscar: The New Kid That May Change Health Insurance. Retrieved October 25, 2015, from http://www.forbes.com/sites/theapothecary/2013/08/19/say-hi-to-oscar-the-new-kid-that-may-change-health-insurance/

[85] Huhman, H. (2015, June 29). 5 Inexpensive Benefits Millennials Value More Than Health Insurance. Retrieved October 25, 2015, from http://www.entrepreneur.com/article/247750

the technology meets the needs of your employees. A website with plenty of information and resources will be good, but an app will be even better. Put the tools in their hands and they will utilize them.

Millennials report that they don't only want benefit plans that will cover the costs of their care, they want ways to keep themselves healthy. Pay attention here, because wellness programs can pay off hugely for both employees and their employers. Healthier workers means less sick days, greater productivity and generally happier people. It will also mean that the cost of providing coverage to these people will decline, and you can even see fewer worker's compensation injuries.[86] Considering that the costs of implementing a wellness program can be relatively low, this is an easy call.

What should a wellness program look like? Firstly, promote healthy behaviors. Oscar provides monetary rewards for subscribers who take a certain number of steps each day, and it's tracked on a wearable device.[87] Many companies sponsor events that kill two birds with one stone, such as organizing charity walks that get the employees involved in physical activities and burnish their corporate social responsibility reputation. In some areas, local farmers are partnering with companies to bring produce into the workplace, including providing education to the workers about eating healthy, and giving out recipes. Talk to your benefits providers about what kind of wellness incentives they are able to bring to the table. Many are more than happy to send experts who can talk to people about how to use their benefits wisely and provide information about living in a healthful way.

The other side of that coin is inspiring people to give up unhealthy habits. If you have vending machines around your offices, consider taking

[86] Berry, L., Mirabito, A., & Baun, W. (2010, December 1). What's the Hard Return on Employee Wellness Programs? Retrieved October 25, 2015, from https://hbr.org/2010/12/whats-the-hard-return-on-employee-wellness-programs
[87] Griffith, E. (2014, December 9). How is Oscar, the hipster health insurance company, performing? Retrieved October 25, 2015, from http://fortune.com/2014/12/09/oscar-health-insurance/

them out and replacing them with fresh fruit for purchase. Some companies have chosen to offer employees lower premiums for being non-smokers, and encouraging use of smoking cessation programs. Starting a support group for workers who want to lose weight can lead to people taking more walks on their lunch breaks and sharing strategies for eating healthy.

Take a look around at the work environment itself. Is it the kind of place you'd want to be? Sitting under fluorescent lights is not only a total drag (speaking from experience here), it can have a direct effect on health. Poor lighting contributes to eye strain and workplace accidents. It can cause employees' posture to suffer as they crane their necks over their work to see better.[88] It's also common knowledge that happy people are healthy people. Bring color into the design of the space. Add a few plants, and give people access to a window. We aren't gerbils. Actually, even gerbils need a stimulating environment if they're going to last any appreciable amount of time.

Another key piece of being well is not just allowing, but encouraging employees to use their paid time off. Workers who take vacations are not only more productive, but research shows that they are more likely to be promoted than their peers who do not.[89] Mental health is as important a part of wellness as physical health, and smart companies recognize this. Some have even begun to switch over to the Unlimited PTO model, a benefit that many Millennials report valuing highly.[90]

I am imagining what you might be saying into the pages of this book. "Whoa, hold on. I was with you about the wellness program, but

---

[88] Lighting In Offices. (2003, December 1). Retrieved October 25, 2015, from http://www.labour.gov.hk/eng/public/oh/OHB50.pdf
[89] Yankowicz, W. (2015, June 15). Why You Need to Encourage Employees to Use Their Vacation Time. Retrieved October 25, 2015, from http://www.inc.com/will-yakowicz/4-reasons-why-you-need-to-encourage-employees-use-vacation.html
[90] Taurasi, L. (2015, June 3). 8 Great Employee Benefits Millennials Actually Want. Retrieved October 25, 2015, from http://workplace.care.com/8-great-employee-benefits-millennials-actually-want

unlimited time off? Who would want to work if they didn't have to?" For some reason, when people hear about this benefit they immediately envision all the employees who will just take a month-long vacation every quarter, because hey, they're entitled to it. Slow down, it's not all that crazy.

The foundation of any paid time off program, including an unlimited plan, is a well-written policy. Truly, the only unlimited aspect of the paid time off should be the annual allotment, but there should indeed be limitations on how much time can be requested at once, other than a leave of absence situation. It should stipulate how far in advance requests must be made, and of course that approval will be based on appropriate coverage for the needs of the business. Absenteeism, both of frequency and pattern, will still be against the rules and dealt with through a progressive discipline process. It's not an anything goes situation.

With that policy, employees now have much more flexibility. Take, for example, a company that offers five paid sick days per year. If I get the flu, I could easily exhaust all five days in one shot, and I'll be left hoping that I don't get food poisoning or any other acute illness for the rest of my time. What if my child gets the flu, and I'm out taking care of her? If she uses all my five days, I'm crossing my fingers that I somehow manage to never get sick. Never. An unlimited policy means that these situations don't cause me to lose out on a paycheck.

I should insert a giant disclaimer here: an unlimited PTO policy is not for every workplace. If your management hierarchy won't be able to handle the appropriate oversight, meaning that they will keep watch over what gets used and take action when needed, you're setting yourself up for disaster. If there is an inherent lack of trust between the workers and the company, this is not the perk for you. You should certainly address those issues, and maybe afterward it can be considered.

All of this should look somewhat familiar: Millennials are looking for the two-way street. Their lives are about much more than coming and going from work. It's also about ensuring that the years of their lives are quality years. It's about taking care of a company through exceptional work, and being taken care of in return. You may also take note that the expectations we have of employers often mirror what we came to expect from our parents. When it came time to choose a college, we were taken to college fairs, supported as we poured over leaflets and brochures, and taken on as many campus visits as we needed. We were given all of the assistance we needed to make the right decision for us, and we're carrying that expectation into work.

This is where the myth of the Millennial who needs to constantly be parented is actually accurate, but I reject that it is a negative mark on our record. If you are offering such complex products and health benefits and investment portfolios to your employees, why would you not want them to be well-informed about it? We're openly telling you that we want information so we can make the most of what you are giving us, so don't turn away from us. I've seen companies that bemoan low participation rates, and I point the finger right back at them when I note that they aren't providing anything to their employees to encourage their participation other than a booklet and an enrollment form. This proposition has now become a partnership, so the time is now to step it up and get in the game.

You may have noticed my mention of the desire for technology in making benefit choices, and your eyes may have rolled. Great, another reason for them to be surgically attached to their phones. Well, yes, we do love our devices, and as time goes on we're being offered more to carry and wear. However, the outlook isn't as bad as you may think, and the problem may not just be us. Let's take a look in depth into what exactly we are dealing with.

Myth #6: Millennials are Digital Addicts

"If you do want to hate on Millennials, at least do them the credit of hating them for the right reasons." – Charles Ingraham

Of the technological advances of my generation, perhaps most revolutionary of all is the mobile phone. Although there were many portable communication devices, starting with a military-use walkie talkie in 1938, the first equipment that began to resemble a cell phone was prototyped in 1973. It was huge and awkward, but it made a phone call and needed no wires. Ten years later a somewhat sleeker model hit stores, at a price point of $4,000, boasting then-blazing 1G service. It was available to consumers, but for a long time this type of device was something that only the richest could afford and use regularly.[91] In the 1990 film *Pretty Woman* there is a brief scene of a businessman driving through the ritzy part of L.A. on his giant portable phone, a symbol of status and wealth.

By 1999, phones had been shrinking in size and price point, and Nokia's era of dominance was cemented. Their 3210 model was the most popular unit of its time, selling 160 million handsets. It came in pretty colors. You could make high-quality phone calls and send rapid-fire texts. It had Snake, the original time-wasting game. Critically, it was sold at a price point that made it affordable for younger audiences, and we were hooked.[92]

---

[91] Meyers, J. (2011, May 6). Watch The Incredible 70-Year Evolution Of The Cell Phone. Retrieved July 2, 2015, from http://www.businessinsider.com/complete-visual-history-of-cell-phones-2011-5?op=1
[92] O'Reilly, Q. (2015, May 12). Happy 150th birthday Nokia. Here's why we owe so

The equipment developed at a breakneck pace from here, growing to include cameras, GPS capabilities, web browsers (although the price for data was astronomical) and full keyboards. The next big game changer was the Sidekick, released in 2002.[93] With previously unheard of screen size, a full keyboard and cool style, it was a great device, but its ubiquity among the young celebrity set made it a cornerstone of pop culture. It is what made a cell phone a must-have device.[94]

Next came the Blackberry, which some lovingly referred to as Crackberry, indicating how addictive the device was to use. The Motorola RAZR came next, which brought a new level of design sensibility to an often utilitarian-looking item. Palm brought full PDA capabilities with its devices, but the apotheosis of frenzied cell-fanaticism came in 2007.[95]

When Steve Jobs introduced the very first iPhone, he said it "is like having your life in your pocket."[96] You could view the internet as it really was, and not just a mobile version of a page. It made phone calls. It texted beautifully. It had all these funky little widgets we'd come to know as apps. And it did all of that in an absolutely gorgeous package. How could we not be seduced?

The rest is our present-day history. We are now living in an age of near-total digital saturation. It's hard to think of anyone in our social

much to the 3210. Retrieved July 2, 2015, from http://businessetc.thejournal.ie/nokia-150-birthday-3210-2098454-May2015/

[93] Meyers, J. (2011, May 6). Watch The Incredible 70-Year Evolution Of The Cell Phone. Retrieved July 2, 2015, from http://www.businessinsider.com/complete-visual-history-of-cell-phones-2011-5?op=1

[94] Hollister, S. (2011, May 31). Danger's iconic Hiptop fades away / the Sidekick is here to stay. Retrieved July 2, 2015, from http://www.engadget.com/2011/05/31/dangers-iconic-hiptop-fades-away-the-sidekick-is-here-to-stay/

[95] Meyers, J. (2011, May 6). Watch The Incredible 70-Year Evolution Of The Cell Phone. Retrieved July 2, 2015, from http://www.businessinsider.com/complete-visual-history-of-cell-phones-2011-5?op=1

[96] Transcript – iPhone Keynote 2007. (n.d.). Retrieved July 2, 2015, from http://www.european-rhetoric.com/analyses/ikeynote-analysis-iphone/transcript-2007/

network (and I mean the physical one) that doesn't at least have an internet-capable phone. The Pew Research Center noted that sixty-four percent of Americans have a smartphone. Not just a cell phone – a *smartphone*. The devices have become so inexpensive (premium gadgets notwithstanding) that the barrier to entering this level of communication and accessibility to information is very low. There are many positives to this, such as helping to spread the availability of internet access to people who might not be able to purchase a computer, which represents seven percent of users.[97] For all the upsides, though, we've all seen the negatives.

I, myself, have been incredibly frustrated when walking behind someone who insists that they can walk and text at the same time – you can, but you're not doing either one very well. Texting and driving is becoming a leading cause of motor vehicle collisions.[98] Frustratingly, plenty of people are surfing through news articles, playing the latest freemium app game or browsing through Facebook gossip when they should be working, and it's not just about productivity. So many phones are capable of recording video and sound that business owners have to worry equally about privacy and confidentiality. Users can access inappropriate content while they're wasting your time, and frequently do, exposing your workforce to a potentially hostile work environment. There are plenty of reasons to detest this behavior, and more often than not, the finger is pointed at Generation Y as the biggest offenders in this category.

For this generation, technology is a utility. Imagine your water service: you go to your kitchen, turn on the tap and the water comes out. It's not something most people would be impressed by anymore, we just expect it. The only time you'll hear anyone talking about their water

---

[97] Smith, A. (2015, April 1). U.S. Smartphone Use in 2015. Retrieved July 2, 2015, from http://www.pewinternet.org/2015/04/01/us-smartphone-use-in-2015/
[98] 46 Important Texting While Driving Fatalities Statistics. (2015, March 31). Retrieved July 2, 2015, from http://healthresearchfunding.org/46-important-texting-driving-fatalities-statistics/

service is when it's disrupted. It's the same for our electronics. We don't think twice that our cell phones have more computing power than past moon missions. We don't care that we are able to use a device the size of an ice cream sandwich to call someone in Azerbaijan. We care that our favorite site is taking more than a couple of seconds to load. In fact, statistics reveal that for every second a user waits for an app or webpage to respond, seven percent of them will give up and abandon it.[99] After four seconds you've lost almost thirty percent of your audience's attention span.

It's easy to see how this can extend to the workplace, especially considering that level of engagement is low nationwide. If someone's getting bored at work, they have a personalized, ready-in-an-instant distraction machine at their disposal. The youngest workers report overwhelmingly that they pick up their phones when they are bored – ninety-three percent. Users aged fifty and older are doing so around fifty-five percent of the time.[100] Here's something our generation has to own – we are definitely wasting more time at work on our phones than our older colleagues. Here's the rub: everyone's doing it. Each generation reports blowing off work to fool around on our phones, spending no less than an average of forty minutes per day doing so.[101] If your employees are not engaged with their work, this could be a culprit of widespread cell phone use when they should be working.

I'll take this moment to make a brief confession: I was a serial time waster at work. It's probably safe for me to tell this story now, since I'm no longer employed at this particular organization. I spent plenty of

[99] Oberoi, A. (2014, March 21). 5 Reasons Visitors Leave Your Website. Retrieved July 2, 2015, from http://www.websitemagazine.com/content/blogs/posts/archive/2014/03/21/5-reasons-visitors-leave-your-website.aspx

[100] Smith, A. (2015, April 1). U.S. Smartphone Use in 2015. Retrieved July 2, 2015, from http://www.pewinternet.org/2015/04/01/us-smartphone-use-in-2015/

[101] Conner, C. (2013, September 7). Who Wastes The Most Time At Work? Retrieved July 2, 2015, from http://www.forbes.com/sites/cherylsnappconner/2013/09/07/who-wastes-the-most-time-at-work/

my work hours staring at my phone. No one ever noticed, and I was never disciplined for it. Why? I was terribly bored. I finished every task my supervisor gave me quickly, and even though I asked for more work, there wasn't much more to be done. I should have either been redistributed within the company or let go – if I didn't have enough to do to fill my day, what was the need for the position?

Here's the worst part – I didn't even enjoy it. Staring at my phone for long stretches wasn't what I wanted to be doing. I wanted to be given a task that would force me to test my limits, to spend extra time after work finishing, to be relied upon. I am happy to say that I no longer have to pass the time on my phone. I have a job that engages me fully, and when I look up to see what time it is I'm shocked to find out the day is almost over. I love what I do, and my Netflix queue has never been so neglected.

This is a significant stumbling block that companies need to be able to address. How do we get workers to put the phone down and get back to work? Of course, a well-written policy is important, and just as important is its consistent application, but it's far better to take a proactive approach. Address the reasons that people engage in the negative behavior rather than simply trying to punish it away. How do we do so while simultaneously embracing technology to attract Generation Y and drive business? Enter the internal social network.

There is a valuable lesson in the history of social networking that reveals why this has become such an important medium for Millennials. The company formerly known as America Online, in addition to being the progenitor of Instant Messenger, had a Member Profiles feature, representing the first time people on the internet could share details about themselves for a worldwide audience. The first social network of the kind we'd recognize, launched in 2002, was Friendster, which not only allowed people to talk about themselves, but connect with others and friends-of-friends. At its peak it boasted three million members.[102] It's

---

[102] The history of social networking. (2014, August 4). Retrieved July 2, 2015, from

surprising to note that LinkedIn launched only a year later, but wouldn't find its foothold until much later.

The far bigger launch of 2003 was MySpace. This wasn't just a page to describe yourself and talk to others, but rather a platform of self-expression. You could design the background, add music, sparkly graphics and personal messages. One of the more controversial features of the site was the Top 8, where you sorted who were your eight top friends, and prominently displayed it on the site. There was a fair amount of gossip and social capital spent trying to get into people's Top 8. The popularity of the site was short-lived, however, not because it wasn't great, but because someone came along and did it better.

That someone was Mark Zuckerberg. Himself a Millennial, he created a place where his university classmates could learn about and meet one another. Perhaps what made Facebook popular at first wasn't the product itself, but rather the good fortune of timing the release of it when people were primed to want it. By starting with his own campus, then expanding to other schools, then reaching outside of educational institutions, the product just rode the wave.[103] The site now enjoys an international prestige and billions of users.

Twitter created another paradigm shift upon its launch in 2006. With just 140 characters of space, users were forced to distill their thoughts down to the essence, taking the speed of texting and opening it up to a worldwide audience. What has made the platform a game changer is how it has been leveraged by its users to spread news not covered by traditional journalism.[104] The world had a front-row seat to the Green Revolution of Iran thanks to the pictures, videos and reports posted to the site by the very people participating in it. Gonzo journalism to the extreme.

---

http://www.digitaltrends.com/features/the-history-of-social-networking/
[103] Phillips, S. (2007, July 25). A brief history of Facebook. Retrieved July 2, 2015, from http://www.theguardian.com/technology/2007/jul/25/media.newmedia
[104] Johnson, M. (2013, January 23). The History of Twitter. Retrieved July 2, 2015, from http://www.socialnomics.net/2013/01/23/the-history-of-twitter/

As the industry developed, the number of networks has exploded. We can now choose from Instagram, Snapchat, Kik, Yik Yak, Snapchat, Vine, Periscope, and each with their own gimmicks. Companies have realized the incredible value to be had in how they can connect with their customers, and it's a natural conclusion that they can connect in similar ways with their workers.

Many employers have jumped on this particular bandwagon, with recent statistics revealing over half of companies offering this communication platform.[105] It sounds great on its face – build your version of Twitter and let the networking and idea-sharing commence. Build it and they will come. They don't automatically come, though, and a useless network can actually be a negative. As with any type of change, to really get the most out of this platform, senior leadership must also be engaged to realize success. Get your CEO to share a key piece of news with the staff. Ask the CFO to post updates on progress toward revenue goals. That's not just a social media secret, that's good for engagement – employees who feel aligned to the company's mission and goals are more engaged with their work, no matter their generation.[106]

If your employees see that this is a network the company intends to drive, they will see value in it. As a bonus, your Millennial employees will be thrilled with the opportunity to view the thoughts of executives and respond – they report wanting access to executives early and regularly, and feel they have valuable ideas to share.[107] Beyond that, if a worker finds themselves bored and a vibrant social network is available to

[105] Gose, C. (2013, May 30). More than half of companies use social media for internal communication. Retrieved July 2, 2015, from http://www.rmgnetworks.com/blog/bid/292598/More-than-half-of-companies-use-social-media-for-internal-communication

[106] Straz, M. (2014, December 8). Make a New Year's Resolution to Align Employee Success With Company Goals. Retrieved July 2, 2015, from http://www.entrepreneur.com/article/240498

[107] Stahl, A. (2015, June 4). Managing Millennials: Six Musts For CEOs Who Want To Get Ahead. Retrieved July 2, 2015, from http://www.forbes.com/sites/ashleystahl/2015/06/04/managing-millennials-6-musts-for-ceos-who-want-to-get-ahead/

them that centers around what they do, they may very well spend that time connecting with colleagues in other departments on cross-functional ideas, or simply getting to know others better.

The love of technology has led this generation to some radical ideas about what the traditional workplace is, and how it functions. Just as one expects to be able to access their personal email from anywhere on earth, they feel they can do the same with work email. Needing access to a phone is no longer a valid reason to keep people at a desk. In fact, JP Morgan Chase dispensed with voicemail entirely for many of their employees.[108] We've noticed that being at our desks is really not a necessity for us to be productive, so if the only reason we should be there is because it's what has always been done, we won't cotton to that. Given the opportunity to be flexible with our work schedules, we will make sure that our work fits our lives,[109] and while that might not take place in plain view, it doesn't mean that it isn't happening.

It will be well worth any manager's time to devise a different way to measure productivity than simply the amount of time a person sits in their desk. Quantify your expectations, and share that with your employees. Put deadlines on deliverables, and have regular check-ins with your team, both in a group and separately. If your employee seems to roll through everything and still have extra time, give them a project to challenge them. Not only will it give you something extra to advance your department's goals, but it will demonstrate some additional areas where this person might be ready to develop. And if you're finding yourself annoyed that your worker goes home at a nice hour each night, maybe you need to delegate a bit more. If you're finding that a hard pill to swallow, it may come down to trust. If you don't feel you can trust your

---

[108] Sweet, K. (2015, June 3). JPMorgan Chase getting rid of voicemail for some employees. Retrieved July 2, 2015.

[109] Schulte, B. (2015, May 5). Millennials want a work-life balance. Their bosses just don't get why. Retrieved July 2, 2015, from http://www.washingtonpost.com/local/millennials-want-a-work-life-balance-their-bosses-just-dont-get-why/2015/05/05/1859369e-f376-11e4-84a6-6d7c67c50db0_story.html

team, you either need a better team or you need to be able to let go and feel confident that others can get the job done just as well as you.

There are other gains to be had with allowing people to be flexible. If you allow workers to share their workspaces, spending some of their time telecommuting, the company can save on real estate costs, not to mention all the ancillary costs of not having to maintain a space with so many employees.[110] This is a win-win that makes for a great perk for employees, and will give Millennials, who work to live rather than the reverse, a great reason to stick around. In the end, people are all different, and while some people will gleefully show up at eight o'clock to start a very productive morning, others find their creativity and best productivity at eleven at night. The company that allows people to work when they know they work best will get the most out of each person.

Still need convincing? Generation Y wants workplace flexibility because they are more likely to be in a partnership with a full-time worker, and because they have largely delayed having children until their late twenties and early thirties, they are reaching management positions at a time when they are just building their families. Millennials would relocate, even to a different country, to get better flexibility. They'd take a pay cut[111] – so much for the thought of us leaving for the bigger paycheck.

So, yes, we are digitally addicted, but I think it's safe to say we all are, and it's not hard to see why. The last thirty years have seen advancements in the technological and social space at a pace that no one could have predicted, and has not yet slowed. The next big fad is just around the corner, and it will bring opportunities that we will love, but new reasons to be annoyed as well. Smart leaders won't just adapt to one

---

[110] Meister, J. (2013, April 1). Flexible Workspaces: Employee Perk Or Business Tool To Recruit Top Talent? Retrieved July 2, 2015, from http://www.forbes.com/sites/jeannemeister/2013/04/01/flexible-workspaces-another-workplace-perk-or-a-must-have-to-attract-top-talent/
[111] Fondas, N. (2015, May 7). Millennials Say They'll Relocate for Work-Life Flexibility. Retrieved July 2, 2015, from https://hbr.org/2015/05/millennials-say-theyll-relocate-for-work-life-flexibility

and be satisfied – they will keep their companies nimble to adjust, and have the foresight to see which will be worth their time and which will simply be the next Google+.

Advice for Millennials

The moral of the story so far, if I had to put one forward, is that the emergence of the Millennial generation is not as seismic as it has been made out to be. It just represents the same kind of social evolution that we've been going through for centuries. The histrionics aren't unusual, but they are unnecessary. The older generations need to stop hyperventilating about classifying or qualifying us and just observe us for who we are. We are neither the slackers nor saviors that we've been held up as, but rather a new definition of average. Among us you will find the amazing and ordinary, the outstanding and unremarkable.

Just like any other group of average people, though, Millennials could use some advice. There are some traits that we tend to possess, and some behaviors we engage in, that only make the challenge of acceptance worse. I would like to provide some thoughts on this, and caution anyone reading this that not all members of Generation Y will fit the description, nor does this exclude people of any generation from taking it.

Put Down the Phone

I get it, you are good at multitasking. You can bang out a text to someone while you're listening to me and do both equally well. I am guilty of it as well, but we can't forget that showing respect to someone comes in many forms, and the courtesy of your full attention is something that anyone will respond positively to. Just as I wouldn't pick my nose in public, even though I can do that and talk to someone at the same time, there are some things that you just shouldn't do. If you are talking to a teacher, a colleague, or anyone from whom you are expecting respect and kindness, put the phone down, even if you can do both.

By the way, you are not as good at multitasking as you think you are. No one is – you're constantly taking attention from one thing to switch to another, and back again just as quickly. You will never be able to do two things at once as well as you could do them separately.[112] Stop lying to yourself and either admit that you're only halfway doing each thing or put one of them down. You could even ask the person you want to speak to for a moment to finish your text so you can be sure to give them your full attention. It probably won't be thrilling to be second fiddle to your device, but at the very least you are acknowledging that they will be your sole focus in a moment. It's better than trying to have a conversation with the top of someone's head.

Earn the Right to Speak About Something

Dale Carnegie, writer of *How to Win Friends and Influence People* and developer of a popular educational series on effective speaking and relationships, has taught that one must earn the right to speak on a subject before they do so. What this means is knowing your subject so well, either through your own experience or a rigorous course of study, that you really know your stuff. While I admire people who want to talk about how to improve the order of business from the moment they finish orientation, we often try to do so without earning the right to have that conversation. This causes a lot of friction with the members of the older generations who see us as upstarts who don't have the experience to know all the variables that they'd like to change.

If you see a better way of doing things, or want to make suggestions to leaders, ask some questions first. Start with your new peers. Find out why things happen the way they do at that time. You may find out that the company tried to make big changes previous to your

---

[112] Hamilton, J. (2008, October 2). Think You're Multitasking? Think Again. Retrieved October 29, 2015, from http://www.npr.org/templates/story/story.php?storyId=95256794

arrival and they failed miserably. When you first walk in the door, you don't know what you don't know about the history of the organization, and you're just starting to learn the culture. An important part of managing change is knowing both, as they will be big factors in how to shake up the status quo, and whether doing so will lead to success.

It's the same as if you saw someone on the street carrying a very heavy bag and you suggest they buy a cart to help them move their belongings. How do you know they haven't already tried it? Maybe the bag wouldn't fit in the cart. Maybe they had a cart but it just broke under the weight of the load, so they had to ditch it in a dumpster. Now you're standing in front of them with a lecture to accompany their sore back. You're not going to influence anyone like that.

Once you do have that institutional knowledge and you're ready to make a suggestion, make sure your delivery is measured. Remember, managers and leaders consider their businesses or departments to be very close to their hearts. Treat the conversation delicately, and don't be a jerk.

Be Each Other's Cheerleaders

In my research for this book I came across so many articles detailing how Millennials are distancing themselves from each other and their generational label. That is even more disappointing to me than the reactions of the people we are rebelling against. We've been hearing a lot of negativity about ourselves, and it seems that we've been internalizing it.

What we've forgotten is that we as individuals are not responsible for representing what wonderful people our cohort can be. That's far too much pressure. You can only be responsible for your own success, and try to bring your peers along with you for the ride, but ultimately they will need to make their way in the world for themselves. Don't fall victim to that old conversation that starts, "Your generation is so..." Stand up for yourself by replying, "Well, I can only speak for myself." List all of your great attributes, and you can even throw in that the people you choose to surround yourself with are just as talented and multi-dimensional. You probably won't change that person's mind, but you will change your own, and that is more important.

The older generations aren't suffering from any of this self-shaming, and just like us they consist of great people and terrible people in the same ratio. Yet somehow the balance of confidence is completely out of control. The Pew Research Center indicated that Millennials were far more likely to rate the cohort's positive traits lower and negative traits higher. For example, only twenty-four percent of Generation Y respondents agreed that the group is responsible. On the other hand, seventy-three percent of the Silent Generation respondents agreed, so they clearly are not having the crisis that we are. Even worse, Millennials were more likely than any other group to say their generation is greedy, self-absorbed, wasteful and cynical.[113] We are our own worst critics.

Frankly, the labels we've been given and seem to have adopted aren't even true. For example, if we are so greedy, then I'm finding it hard to reconcile with the fact that eight-four percent of Millennials donated to charity in 2014. Seventy percent have spent an hour or more doing volunteer work.[114] Does that sound greedy to you?

I believe that part of the problem is that we are still using other generations' definitions for these words. If we're saying Millennials are irresponsible because they haven't bought homes and had children yet, that isn't something we'd use as a yardstick. We'd consider ourselves responsible because we're able to hold down jobs (once we get them) and recognize when it's time to seek out other opportunities to reach our

---

[113] Most Millennials Resist the 'Millennial' Label. (2015, September 3). Retrieved October 29, 2015, from http://www.people-press.org/2015/09/03/most-millennials-resist-the-millennial-label/

[114] Schulte, B. (2015, June 24). Millennials are actually more generous than anybody realizes. Retrieved October 30, 2015, from https://www.washingtonpost.com/news/wonkblog/wp/2015/06/24/millennials-are-actually-more-generous-than-anybody-realizes/

goals. What responsibility looks like to us is not what it looks like to our forebears, and that's causing the misalignment of the impression. Further, that negative stereotype is perpetuating itself in every news article, television expose and tut-tutting business book. This has to stop now.

We need to be willing to challenge people in this area in the same way we'd be able to challenge them in any other. We've been given prizes and ribbons for very little in the past, and as soon as that praise is withheld we fall to pieces. We need to learn to give that praise to ourselves, and each other.

Give Your Boss A Chance

If you are finding yourself dissatisfied in your current role and about to seek out a new one, take a moment to give the situation some thought before you jump. Whether it's a lack of career, money or a bad manager that's causing you to think about leaving, consider letting someone at your current company know first. Many situations don't improve without someone who is willing to speak up about it, and since we're so good at calling out needed improvements, we should do so if our jobs are not satisfactory.

Some problems don't have viable solutions that are immediately knowable from where we sit. You could be sitting in a role where you see no career path whatsoever, but if you were to bring it up to your manager, you may find out the company would be willing to expand your role so you can acquire new skills, even if an obvious next step isn't there. The trust between you and your manager, or the leadership of the company, is what will make the decision for you. If you are in a company that you can't trust, and being frank would only mean trouble for you or your job, then you have to do what's necessary to protect your prospects (I also don't blame you for wanting to leave).

The jump to the next position is always enticing, because the many things you don't know about the new company become all the most amazing and wonderful things you can think of. It's human nature – we tend to assume the best will await us on that greener grass, especially when the company courting us has just told us all of the most wonderful aspects of working there. They don't exactly put the problems on the front page (nor do we). However, making a so-so situation better in your current company may turn out to be a more advantageous move than rolling the dice on an unknown venture. In addition to showing stability, you may get more than you thought you would, and you won't lose your tenure.

This, I think, will also go halfway toward the older generations who think we're ungrateful. Let's agree that, where prudent, we will give our employers a chance to make us happy before we jump ship. If we expect transparency from them, we should be willing to do the same *for* them.

Inherent in this conversation is the suggestion that we need to occasionally trust the people who employ us to help guide us in our careers. It won't always be your manager. You may need to do some networking to find out who the wisest people are to mentor you, and once you find him or her, keep in touch as you move on. Remember what your experience was like, because one day someone may come to you looking for guidance.

Don't Give Up

Although I do own that cynical descriptor, especially when thinking about my financial future, I think we should remain optimistic. As the tide of the job market turns, we will see employers no longer in complete and total control of what we are offered. Companies will once again need to differentiate themselves with competitive salaries and attractive benefits to ensure the best and brightest come to their doors, and we will reap the rewards.

For those of you in college or about to enter college, the time to be diligent is now. Your education will have its place, but keep in mind all of the rich experiences you can gain outside of the classroom that will be just as critical to your future. Seek out and demand opportunities to spend time in the workforce in the field of your choice before you graduate. If you worry that your chosen major isn't going to be the right one for your future job, don't be ashamed to change course if needed. It is far better to redouble your efforts for a profession that will get you paid than one that you love but leaves you unable to support yourself. If you're not completely sure that college is for you, you might be right.

For those of us out of college and in a job that doesn't pay the bills or make you happy, polish up that resume. Make sure your LinkedIn profile is filled with all of your great accomplishments and completely up to snuff. Buy a great interviewing outfit (two if you can – you might get called back for another round) and start practicing your skills. There are a few things I recommend anyone have ready for that next great interview opportunity:

1.   A two-minute description of you for the dreaded "Tell me about yourself" question, including your professional and educational experience and why this job is perfect for you.
2.   A story that talks about how you overcame a significant obstacle and turned it into a positive.
3.   A story about when you took a project or task and totally knocked it out of the park.
4.   All of the things you've already done that the job will require, if you have done them, showing how you will be able to be effective on the job quickly.
5.   Your 90-day plan for your role, if you should get it.

Whatever they end up asking you, you will have a story that will fit the bill. It will help you to remain cool under pressure. If you can manage some interview practice with a friend who might ask you some practice questions, all the better. If you don't know anyone with the skills to help you practice, create a great professional social media profile, or a killer resume, look me up on LinkedIn. For better or for worse, I've never been able to turn down someone who genuinely wants the help and wants to work together to improve. But I'm not going to sugar coat my advice, and if your previous mentors or helpers do, they're not worth keeping in your network.

A critical step that many people forget, but that must be done, is scrubbing all your social media profiles to ensure that they present the type of person that you would want your future employer to see. Get rid of the inappropriate college party pics, the questionable content, and anything that could cause you to lose the position. I can hear the collective complaints of many of my generation, all simultaneously crying out that they should be able to be one person in private and one person at work. Whether that's true or not, you can't. The person that you choose to be in your private life is not only a reflection on who you might be at work, but the line between work and recreation is constantly being blurred, and that's thanks to us. We're very willing to check emails after work, take calls from home and generally conduct business at any hour. Is it really that odd to think that your prospective employer would want you to be a responsible, trustworthy person even when you're away from your desk? Curate a personal brand that represents the great person that you are, and it will be valuable to you not only as a professional, but in your personal life of volunteering and community involvement.

Another factor to consider is how enormously and quickly a personal indiscretion can become an absolute nightmare for the companies they work for. Need I remind you of #HasJustineLandedYet? For those of you who may not recall, Justine Sacco was a Public Relations director at InterActiveCorp in 2013. She made a seriously ill-advised, blatantly racist comment on Twitter to her approximately two hundred followers, then got on an eleven-hour plane ride.[115] While this was only intended for two hundred pairs of eyes, the platform allows readers to Retweet these statements to their own followers, and it multiplies exponentially from there. In fact, this particular tweet became well-known because it was

---

[115] Vingiano, A. (2013, December 21). This Is How A Woman's Offensive Tweet Became The World's Top Story. Retrieved November 2, 2015, from http://www.buzzfeed.com/alisonvingiano/this-is-how-a-womans-offensive-tweet-became-the-worlds-top-s#.fc0yOwX5X

screen-captured and emailed to someone in the online publishing world, and it didn't take long to be seen by millions.

While Justine jetted among the clouds from London to South Africa, blissfully unaware of the unmitigated disaster unfolding miles below her, the Twitterverse, as they are known, made that tweet viral. The hashtag #HasJustineLandedYet trended worldwide, including in the very country she was about to land in, making her an immediate villain. Charities leveraged the uproar to direct donations to their websites, which crashed under the deluge of traffic. Gogo, a provider of wi-fi on airplanes, took advantage of the moment for some free marketing. The outrage was swift and total, and by the time Justine landed she was globally-infamous, and shortly thereafter, unemployed.[116]

It is a significant cautionary tale, but one that is difficult to take. There was a time when people could tell off-color jokes to their pals when they were off the clock and it wouldn't make any difference to their jobs. These people did so at a time when publishing our every thought to the public wasn't even an option. We all feel that we have the right to be whoever we are and if we can also do our jobs very well then it shouldn't matter how horrible we are off company property. That time, for better or worse, is over. If you want to say something offensive to someone – which I don't recommend, but if you must – say it to their faces where it can't be recorded, reproduced and used against you. Keep it in the pub.

Did the company that employed her have the right to terminate her for a joke that she never used to represent them, or made during the course of her work? You bet your life they did. Her actions, however innocuous they were intended to be, made her toxic to that company. They had the risk of losing clients and money, so it was the right choice for the business to let her go. Not only that, but the public themselves cried out for her firing. We're going to have to practice what we preach here and be the people that deserve the work, and not simply put on a mask

---

[116] Ibid.

when we walk into the office. Yes, I'm asking us all to be good people. I know how crazy that sounds.

That isn't to say that the company should be the party holding all the cards during the screening process. When you apply for a job, make sure you are interviewing the company as much as they are interviewing you. Know the type of manager you like working with, and the culture you'd prefer. Ask about who your team would be, and any other questions you'd need to determine (to the extent possible) that you will be happy if you got the position. When you get to the office for your appointment (ten minutes early, naturally), take the time to observe the other workers. Does it look more like a Dilbert comic than you'd feel okay working in? Take mental notes on your observations, and imagine what your day-to-day would be like if you worked there. If you jump into a job that isn't perfect for you, neither you nor your new employer will like it.

It has been a long, hard road to keep our heads above water while the economy struggled, but I believe the light at the tunnel is nearing. Don't forget to contribute to your 401(k) once you are earning those lucrative paychecks – retirement will come, and you will need plenty of time to save in order to be ready for it. Then, start thinking about who's coming in the door behind you, because it will not be very long before we'll be orienting them for their internships, minds open, eager hearts ready to learn. Your evolution must never stop.

What's Next? Generation Z

"What's the point in labeling generations, and is it even helpful to the marketing industry that's embraced it? The answer is less clear than it used to be." – Laura Vanderkam, Fortune Magazine

As we've seen throughout this book, there are great lessons to be learned from the context of history, including the history we're creating now. The young people who are watching Millennials entering the workplace, and the elder generations that work with them, are Generation Z. The world is a rapidly changing place, and exploring some of the events that are taking place now will provide some clues to predict how they will change the business world.

One of the major steps on the Generation Z timeline is the global financial crisis. It was the downfall of many businesses, and many more individuals and families experienced instability of disastrous proportions. The eldest members of Generation Z were eight when the crisis hit in earnest, but grew up watching the struggles of how to cope with the new norms of a redefined economic paradigm.

One epidemic that has been worryingly frequent is school shootings. It seems that we hear a news story monthly of a hero teacher intervening with a student gunman, or a crazed person from outside the school choose the most vulnerable targets, to horrifying results. Generation Z is growing up not only seeing this on the news, but playing out on social media, right in front of their faces.

Also practically unavoidable are some of the greatest global cataclysms that recorded history has ever seen. The 2010 Haiti earthquake and the 2011 Tohoku earthquake demonstrated humanity's frailty, and the many environmental disasters we've faced showed that climate change is stalking ever closer and the consequences will be significant for most of the world. Watching the global response to these disasters will be an indelible memory for them.

Generation Z will have grown up in an era of growing unrest in rebellion against authority figures. Massive protests such as the Occupy Movement or the Black Lives Matter movement will have unfolded before their eyes, and so their eyes will have been opened more than their predecessors, and at an earlier age, to the injustices inherent in our society. Internationally, the Arab Spring played out across the Middle East, with varying results by country. The degree to which all of these movements have the capacity to affect change remains to be seen, and will surely be a part of the continuing conversation.

On the brighter side, we are standing on the precipice of major advances in science and technology. A manned mission to Mars is not as far away as once thought, and driverless cars are not far behind. Thanks to current investments in the STEM (science, technology, engineering and math) subjects, the American population will see an increase in the availability of these skills, and public support for projects in this vein will mean a popular push for achievements on par with the moon landing of 1969.

What will all of this mean for their future?

The Changing Value of a College Degree

As I mentioned earlier, Generation Y has accrued a record-setting amount of college debt. It has hindered the group's ability to buy homes, be independent and make a living wage. What's more, that college education was not a guarantee of employment, and the 2008 recession meant a lot of unemployment and underemployment for this group. With crippling bills and few ways to pay it off, this cohort has been squeezed terribly. In fact, for eighty-two percent of students with over $50,000 in student loans, their post-graduation sentiment is that their investment wasn't worth what they paid.[117] For institutions justifying higher tuitions with higher prestige, this should be an alarm call.

Generation Z is paying attention to this, and may be making different decisions than the previous generation. Whereas employers could look for recruits from top colleges as a matter of course, the institution won't matter as much to this generation. Choices that older workers may have considered a plan B, such as community college (which President Obama has pushed to make free or more affordable to thousands of students) or technical schools are now thoughtfully considered alternatives. Leaders making hiring decisions will need to adjust their expectations of where the value of an education is derived to reach the cream of this crop.

Young students are already reporting that they have different expectations of what their university experience will entail. A survey by Northwestern University study reports that the teenagers contemplating college are expecting professional experience to be an important part of the pedagogy, and their schooling should prepare them for real life.[118] In fact, major disciplines that do not provide much in the way of job prospects or practical preparation may begin to decline significantly. Even large corporations like Ernst & Young have realized this, and have stopped requiring all applicants to have college degrees.[119]

Job skills may not always come from the classroom at all. Recruiters and hiring managers will need to begin to evaluate the

---

[117] Kamenetz, A. (2015, September 29). $50,000 In Student Loans? You Probably Don't Think College Was Worth It.

[118] 'Generation Z' is entrepreneurial, wants to chart its own future. (2014, November 18). Retrieved July 17, 2015.

[119] Lucas, S. (2015, September 22). Ernst & Young Stopped Requiring Degrees. Should You? Retrieved October 24, 2015, from http://www.inc.com/suzanne-lucas/ernst-amp-young-stopped-requiring-degrees-should-you.html

readiness of an applicant not based on their education level, but moreso the skills they've acquired, including those that are self-taught. There are so many ways to learn how to code computers that are either low cost or free[120] that it's becoming silly to expect someone to pay a premium just to learn it in an institution that will give you an embossed, cardstock certificate when you're through. A better way to recruit for these positions would be through ways that help you evaluate a candidate's skills before they even put their name on the application. Host a coding competition through your company's social media pages to find the next great worker.

This generation is also the first to be digital native, people who were born after many of the technologies we've had to learn and keep pace with had already been invented. Infants and toddlers are even using iPads, so the idea of technology as a utility that began with Millennials will be even more of a factor in this generation. Companies that have not yet embraced the use of technology as a matter of course will slowly be left behind if they don't find ways to catch up now. Generation Z will expect that fluency with technology and its intelligent deployment is a given. What will really make them sit up and take notice is the ways that companies will utilize it to make lives and work better. The greater the advance, the more value it will have, and this will include wanting to see improvements for society as a whole. This generation believes that there are steps we can take to make the world better, and this will be reflected in their expectations of how corporate social responsibility will evolve.

The New Definition of Diversity

Generation Z will be nearly majority-minority, meaning that white, non-Hispanic individuals will make up only a bare majority of the population.[121] This will mean that, in order to attract and retain this

---

[120] Pinola, M. (2015, February 7). Top 10 Ways to Teach Yourself to Code. Retrieved October 24, 2015, from http://lifehacker.com/top-10-ways-to-teach-yourself-to-code-1684250889
[121] Villa, J. (2015, September 3). Multiracial Gen Z And The Future Of Marketing. Retrieved October 25, 2015, from

generation, they will need to be able to see their own backgrounds reflected in the workplaces they will seek to fill, both in the line staff and in leadership roles. Now is the time to take a look at who is sitting around your conference room tables and in your C-suite offices and determine how you will broaden the spectrum of talent.

Although I don't feel it should be necessary, let me make a brief pitch for promoting diversity in your company. Diverse groups are more creative, productive and engaged. Companies that diversify experience a competitive edge against their peers that do not, and there is no better way for your product or service to connect with a diverse customer base than to make sure your staff reflect the communities they serve.[122] As the world around us becomes more diverse, so must your company in order to remain in the game.

I also posit that the increasing variations in the population at work will mean that encouragement of diversity and prevention of discrimination will begin to take on a different look. In today's workplace we typically seek to define inappropriate behaviors based on the categories they offend in order to make sure we've been compliant in our response. Increasingly, however, the focus will shift away from making sure each person is protected based on their appropriate category to simply ensuring a positive, supportive workplace for everyone. With the rapidly growing list of protected classes on both the state and federal level, we will soon come to a point where no one will be without one or more classes they could fit into. As Generation Z moves into the legislative realm, our laws may evolve to reflect and react to this.

Increasing diversity will also mean seeking out individuals from different socio-economic statuses, which will become more of a reality as

---

http://www.mediapost.com/publications/article/257641/multiracial-gen-z-and-the-future-of-marketing.html

[122] Walter, E. (2014, January 14). Reaping The Benefits Of Diversity For Modern Business Innovation. Retrieved October 25, 2015, from http://www.forbes.com/sites/ekaterinawalter/2014/01/14/reaping-the-benefits-of-diversity-for-modern-business-innovation/

the college degree becomes both less expensive and less necessary to getting a job. It is hoped that this will come with a commensurate increase in upward mobility for people of every background.

In addition, as the voices of Hispanic and African-American populations grows, the values that are deeply held in these cultures will be areas of focus for companies who begin to see these groups become a greater part of their leadership teams. Businesses, and Americans generally, will begin to understand the dramatic degree of diversity that these cultures have within them, and will no longer be able to be understood as monolithic voices. Attracting and retaining these groups will be less about checking a box, and more about being a part of these communities with them.

Learn From Our Fails

Just as Millennials learned a lot about working and making a living from the generations before us, Generation Z is watching my cohort carefully, and learning from our mistakes. Social media profiles will be carefully cultivated examples of personal brand management, having seen the kinds of catastrophes that oversharing on the internet has brought on us. As we were taught by our teachers to craft and maintain an exceptional resume, Generation Z will ensure that their footprint reflects exactly who they want to portray to the world.

Generation Y has failed in one aspect that I am sad to point out – we thought creating a great life would come easy. We were told to get good grades in school, get into a great college, graduate with a degree and a job would be waiting. We were told we could earn a decent salary so we could afford to buy a house, and we could start a family just like our parents did. The harsh realities of the new economy have shown us that we were complacent, and we've had to redouble our efforts just to catch up to where we expected to be at the ages we are now, and we're finding it difficult, if not impossible.

The next generation knows this, and they are already buckling down for a fight for what they want. They are realistic about the challenges of surviving and thriving both in their lives and at work, and are ready to face them head-on. They will surely be a more cautious group, taking our optimism as a cautionary tale. We will see them more prepared for the rigors of the new normal, and be better prepared to move out, own homes and start families than we were able to be.

This will also likely be paired with a turn away from the ever-escalating arms race of shock and spectacle that our society seems to be steeped in, such as the antics of today's pop and hip hop stars. Just as the 90's reacted to the outrageous 80's with flannel and stripped down rock, the young generation will respect a return to a reflection of life as it actually is, and not the oversaturated decadence of what we aspire to.

In the workplace, that will mean these employees will value transparency. Be honest on not just the big-picture questions, such as the state of the company and what the challenges are, but also on the small scale ones. A Generation Z worker will want to hear the good, bad and ugly of their performance, so that they can continue to improve where needed and do a great job.

This generation will also be even better hustlers than we are. Whereas we learned in the school of hard knocks, the younger workers will come pre-programmed to bring their A-game to the projects they tackle. Be prepared to give them more general parameters for how you want the work done, and allow them to bring their own innovative spirit to the work. You will not only find they will respond very positively to the initiative, but they will also amaze you what they will come up with.

Traits of the Generation

For many reasons, this cohort will have learned how to be prepared. Whether it's for work, in their personal lives, or simply in how they will deal with day to day stresses, they will be planners. At work they will think ahead on how to accomplish their work, and will appreciate hearing the same from their supervisors. They will think a couple of steps ahead in general, and that will include their careers. I don't foresee an end to the 4.4 year average job tenure.

As the world shrinks thanks to advances in technology and transportation, Generation Z will continue to lead the way in understanding and applying diversity. Bringing an international perspective to work will no longer be a specialization, but rather a matter of course that businesses will gladly be able to take advantage of. Not only will there be a surge in the languages the employee base will be able to speak, but the customer a product can attract will only be increased by the diversity of the group behind it.

In many ways, though, how this generation will act will be unpredictable. Thanks to increasing immigration and diversity, the experiences of the American child will not be the only ones affecting the workplace. The pasts of children from the world over will be brought to the enduring melting pot, and many of the biggest events happening in nations many thousands of miles away will have an impact on people we will one day be managing. Open-mindedness will be the most important tool in our arsenal.

In sum, Millennials had better be prepared. The generation coming in after us will be quicker, more agile, and raise the high bar we've already set on innovation. That's where the reactions usually begin. We don't want to be the next in a long line of generations that somehow ignore all of the great aspects of who a group of people are only to point out their foibles or misunderstand their motives. Let's be the most welcoming generation, and prepare ourselves now to take advantage of all the amazing things our young colleagues will be ready to do.

In Closing

"Stories about the new and exciting ways in which you are likely to suffer more or less in comparison to generations whose experiences you can't possibly co-opt/absorb via osmosis/know innately aren't really going to help you do what you have to do: Be in the world at your intersection on earth and exist the best you can, in spite of this collection of forces working for/against you." – Tracy Moore, Jezebel

If you've ever watched the critically-acclaimed FX series *Louie*, starring Louis C.K., you may have come across an episode that opens in a store run by a Millennial. After being refused help with a product he wanted, the cashier, who turned out to be the owner, gave a speech that was so snarky that it made Louie (and me, if I'm being honest) not want to listen to her. I couldn't stand this person, but it didn't make her wrong. She said:

"We're the future. And you don't belong in it. Because we're beyond you, and naturally, that makes you feel kind of bad. You have this deep-down feeling that you don't matter anymore. You should be glad, though … Do you want your kids' world to be a step above yours? Isn't that what we're all doing? So, doesn't it follow that if you're a good parent, and your kids evolve, and are smarter than you, they're going to make you feel kind of dumb? So if you feel stupid around young people, things are going good."[123]

---

[123] Emami, G. (2015, April 24). This Week's Teachable Moment on Louie: Listen to the Youth, They're Smarter Than You. Retrieved October 13, 2015, from http://www.vulture.com/2015/04/24-year-old-explains-the-future-to-louis-ck.html#

It's hard to listen to a self-important brat, but most especially when she's right, and I hope that I've struck a fair balance between being blunt and being honest. If you've made it this far through the book, thank you. A lot of the myths and beliefs I've deconstructed are closely-held, and often emotionally charged. It is true for my generation, too, that these concepts have inspired a lot of emotions in us, and usually negative ones. Much of what we have heard has made us angry, confused, annoyed, or a mix of all three, and rather than let the conversation go on around us, I thought it was time to become part of it.

I expect that there will be disagreements with some of the assertions I've made, and I will consider that a part of the continuing discourse, a reward for my hard work. The challenge for all of us going forward will be to keep our emotions in check as both sides attempt to coexist and adapt along with our workplaces. But if your response is to simply dig your heels in and refuse to acknowledge that the time to adjust to a new paradigm has come, it really won't matter, anyway. We are going to shape the workplaces around us whether you evolve with us or stand in the corner and pout.

Truthfully, it's not just the entrance of Millennials into the workplace that is creating seismic changes in our working world, but the entire marketplace around us as well. Our devices are more interactive and responsive, so we expect the companies we deal with to do the same. We want to not only be able to purchase a product and walk away happy, but we want that product to be an ongoing conversation with not just the company we purchased it from, but other users as well. Management, therefore, is evolving to meet those changes. Supervisors, and the relationships they have with their subordinates, have to learn how to be more interactive and intuitive to continue to compete in a dynamic landscape.

If you are a business owner or senior leader who has read this book and would like to start taking some action, allow me some time for a plug for my dear profession. The field of Human Resources has come a long way even from my first job, not to mention its inception. No longer are we just the paper pushers, the joy killers and the harassment people. We are now in a position to be a trusted partner with the top officers of our businesses. If you haven't offered your top HR staff a seat at the proverbial table, the time has come to have the conversation that will dramatically change the way your employees engage with your company. We have a lot to offer, and we can't wait to show you.

My last words will be for my fellow generation members. Millennials, I've been with you in the frustration. We've taken a lot of grief for things we didn't feel like we owned or controlled, and we've been pushing back. Pretty soon we'll be in a position where the rubber will meet the road and the time to act on all our ideals and goals will be at hand. I'm going to be working hard to keep my optimism for change, my kumbaya spirit and my bullheaded desire to see the world evolve for the better for everyone. I sincerely hope we all do. Because in ten, twenty and thirty years we'll be judging the next generations, and when the time comes to bring them along into a new world, I will be profoundly disappointed if we've simply sold out.

Kids, don't ever change.

Acknowledgements

I'd like to firstly thank Citation Machine, for making it easy to keep myself honest. Your page is very crashy, though.

Secondly, to all of my friends, relatives and co-workers who have read this work in its various states of completion, you have my gratitude. Your feedback was honest and fair, and it inspired me to keep going. I hope I've done a good job of representing your thoughts and feelings. And if you were anonymously quoted in this book and it sounded like we had some conversation like what you've read, then yes, it's you, but I still love you.

To Marie Waugh, a mentor and friend: without your input I wouldn't have gotten here, both in the sense of the book and my career. The next dinner is on me.

And finally, Bill and Caity. I don't think there is a luckier person on earth than me because of having you two in my life. I'm done working – let's go play!

www.ingramcontent.com/pod-product-compliance
Lightning Source LLC
Chambersburg PA
CBHW060357190526
45169CB00002B/635